CryptoClub

STUDENT CIPHER HANDBOOK

Janet Beissinger | Bonnie Saunders
University of Chicago
University of Illinois Chicago

Kendall Hunt
publishing company

CRYPTOGRAPHY & MATHEMATICS

AF895835

Kendall Hunt
publishing company

www.kendallhunt.com
Send all inquiries to:
4050 Westmark Drive
Dubuque, IA 52004-1840

THE UNIVERSITY OF ILLINOIS AT CHICAGO

UCHICAGO
STEM EDUCATION

This material is based upon work supported by the National Science Foundation under Grant No. 0840313. Any opinions, findings, and conclusions or recommendations expressed in this material are those of the author(s) and do not necessarily reflect the views of the National Science Foundation.

Copyright © 2020 by The Board of Trustees of the University of Illinois and The University of Chicago.

ISBN 978-1-7924-2297-3

All rights reserved. No part of this publication may be reproduced, stored in a retrieval system, or transmitted, in any form or by any means, electronic, mechanical, photocopying, recording, or otherwise, without the prior written permission of the copyright owner. Published in the United States of America.

Contents

Introduction v
Chapter 1: Caesar Ciphers **1**
Exploring Patterns 1 3
Caesar Ciphers: Encrypting and Decrypting—Using a Cipher Table and Cipher Wheel 4
Caesar Ciphers: Encrypting and Decrypting—Using a Vigenère Square 5
Caesar Ciphers: More Encrypting 6
Caesar Ciphers: More Decrypting 7
Caesar Ciphers: Cracking 8
Caesar Ciphers: More Cracking 1 9
Caesar Ciphers: More Cracking 2 10
Chapter 2: Additive Ciphers **11**
Exploring Patterns 2 13
Additive Ciphers: Encrypting 14
Additive Ciphers: More Encrypting 15
Additive Ciphers: Decrypting 16
Additive Ciphers: Decrypting—What Happens When You Get Negative Numbers? 17
Additive Ciphers: More Decrypting 1 18
Additive Ciphers: Decrypting—Making Calculations Simpler 19
Additive Ciphers: More Decrypting 2 20
Additive Ciphers: Cracking 21
Additive Ciphers: More Cracking 1 22
Additive Ciphers: More Cracking 2 23
Chapter 3: Keyword and Other Substitution Ciphers **25**
Exploring Patterns 3 27
Keyword Ciphers: Encrypting and Decrypting 28
Keyword Ciphers: More Encrypting 29
Keyword Ciphers: More Decrypting 30
Keyword Ciphers: Cracking 31
Keyword Ciphers: More Cracking 32
Letter Frequencies: Definitions 33
Letter Frequencies: Examining English Text 34
Letter Frequencies: Sample English Text 35
Substitution Ciphers: Make Your Own Table 36
Substitution Ciphers: Make Your Own Pattern 37
Substitution Ciphers: Cracking—Using Letter Frequencies 38
Chapter 4: Multiplicative Ciphers **39**
Exploring Patterns 4 41
Multiplicative Ciphers: Encrypting 42
Reducing Mod 26: Larger Numbers 43
Reducing Mod 26: Finding Remainders 44
Multiplicative Ciphers: More Encrypting 45
Multiplicative Ciphers: Decrypting—Using Tables 46

Multiplicative Ciphers: Good and Bad Keys . . . 47
Multiplicative Ciphers: Decrypting—Using Inverses . . . 48
Finding Multiplicative Inverses . . . 49
Multiplicative Ciphers: More Decrypting . . . 50
Multiplicative Ciphers: Cracking . . . 51
Multiplicative Ciphers: Cracking—Using Algebra . . . 52
Multiplicative Ciphers: More Cracking 1 . . . 53
Multiplicative Ciphers: More Cracking 2 . . . 54
Chapter 5: Vigenère Ciphers . . . 55
Exploring Patterns 5 . . . 57
Vigenère Ciphers: Encrypting and Decrypting—Using Cipher Wheels . . . 58
Vigenère Ciphers: Encrypting and Decrypting—Using Vigenère Squares . . . 59
Vigenère Ciphers: More Encrypting . . . 60
Vigenère Ciphers: More Decrypting . . . 61
Vigenère Ciphers: Cracking—Part 1 Finding the Keylength . . . 62
Vigenère Ciphers: Cracking—Part 2 Cracking When You Know the Keylength . . . 63
Vigenère Ciphers: More Cracking . . . 64
Chapter 6: Affine Ciphers . . . 65
Exploring Patterns 6 . . . 67
Affine Ciphers: Encrypting . . . 68
Affine Ciphers: More Encrypting . . . 69
Affine Ciphers: Decrypting . . . 70
Affine Ciphers: More Decrypting 1 . . . 71
Affine Ciphers: Encrypting and Decrypting—Using Formulas . . . 72
Affine Ciphers: More Decrypting 2 . . . 73
Affine Ciphers: Cracking . . . 74
Affine Ciphers: Cracking Using Algebra . . . 75
Affine Ciphers: More Cracking 1 . . . 76
Affine Ciphers: More Cracking 2 . . . 77
Appendix: Cryptography Tools and Tables . . . 79
Cipher Tables . . . 81
Cipher Tables for Numbers . . . 82–83
Mod 26 Spiral . . . 84
Letter-to-Number Table and Vigenère Square . . . 85
Blank Grid Paper . . . 86
Cipher Certificate . . . 87–88
Cipher Wheels . . . 89

Introduction

Welcome to CryptoClub!

The purpose of this handbook is to introduce you to several ciphers you can use in games and activities at your CryptoClub meetings. Your club leader will have many more messages to use with these ciphers. Keep this handbook as a reference if you need a reminder.

You can find more messages to encrypt and decrypt and other cryptography activities on the CryptoClub website, *cryptoclub.org*.

Cryptography is the science of sending secret messages. It is has long been used by spies and military personnel to send top secret information. Kids have used it for fun when sending messages to their friends. Today, people use cryptography in their everyday lives—sometimes without even knowing it—as they shop on the Internet, use ATM machines, and watch cable TV. Cryptography is an important part of our modern world.

We hope that while you are in the CryptoClub, you enjoy learning about cryptography and using mathematics. After your CryptoClub sessions are over, we encourage you to continue exploring cryptography on the CryptoClub website.

Chapter 1

Caesar Ciphers

Exploring Patterns 1

1. Figure out the answer to the riddle below. Use the cipher table to show how the letters were encrypted. Find a pattern to complete the cipher table.

What is the clumsiest bee?

B		C	V	N	C	M	J	O	H		C	F	F

Cipher Table

a	b	c	d	e	f	g	h	i	j	k	l	m	n	o	p	q	r	s	t	u	v	w	x	y	z

2. Use the cipher table to decrypt the message below.

U P F O D S Z Q U, X F V T F E U I F D B F T B S D J Q I F S.

Caesar Ciphers: Encrypting and Decrypting

Using a Cipher Table and Cipher Wheel

The cipher used on the previous page was a Caesar cipher with key 1. In a **Caesar cipher**, each letter is replaced by a letter farther along in the alphabet. You can think of it as shifting the alphabet to the left. The **key** of a Caesar cipher is the number of places the alphabet is shifted. Here is the cipher table for a a Caesar cipher with key 3:

Key 3

a	b	c	d	e	f	g	h	i	j	k	l	m	n	o	p	q	r	s	t	u	v	w	x	y	z
D	E	F	G	H	I	J	K	L	M	N	O	P	Q	R	S	T	U	V	W	X	Y	Z	A	B	C

Example 1: Use the table to encrypt and decrypt with key 3.

Encrypt Key 3

plaintext:	h	i	d	d	e	n
CIPHERTEXT:	K					

Decrypt Key 3

plaintext:	t							
CIPHERTEXT:	W	U	H	D	V	X	U	H

A cipher wheel is another way to show how the Caesar cipher shifts the alphabet. The figure shows a cipher wheel with key 4.

Example 2: Use the cipher wheel to encrypt and decrypt with key 4.

Encrypt Key 4

plaintext:	s	e	c	r	e	t
CIPHERTEXT:	W					

Decrypt Key 4

plaintext:	m					
CIPHERTEXT:	Q	I	W	W	E	K	I

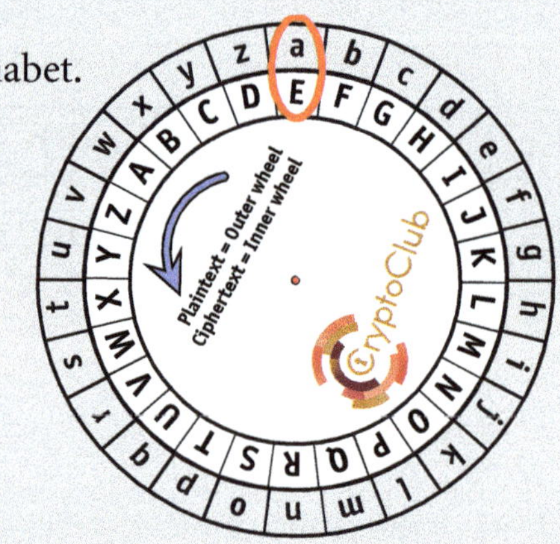

Cipher wheel with key 4

Decrypt the answers to the following riddles. Use a cipher wheel.

1. **Riddle:** What goes up but not down?

   Answer: Key 4

plaintext:														
CIPHERTEXT:	C	S	Y	V		E	K	I						

2. **Riddle:** What is a tree's favorite drink?

   Answer: Key 10

plaintext:														
CIPHERTEXT:	B	Y	Y	D		L	O	O	B					

Caesar Ciphers: Encrypting and Decrypting

Using a Vigenère Square

The **Vigenère square** shows all possible Caesar cipher shifts. Its name comes from a different cipher, the Vigenère cipher. But it is also useful with Caesar ciphers.

To **encrypt:** Begin in the top row with the plaintext letter you want to encrypt. Follow its column down to the row that has the same number as your key. Encrypt with the letter where the row and column meet.

To **decrypt:** Find the ciphertext letter you want to decrypt in the row that has the same number as your key. Follow its column up to the plaintext letter in the top row.

*To encrypt plaintext **t** with key = 3, begin with **t** in the top row.*

	a	b	c	d	e	f	g	h	i	j	k	l	m	n	o	p	q	r	s	t	u	v	w	x	y	z
0	A	B	C	D	E	F	G	H	I	J	K	L	M	N	O	P	Q	R	S	T	U	V	W	X	Y	Z
1	B	C	D	E	F	G	H	I	J	K	L	M	N	O	P	Q	R	S	T	U	V	W	X	Y	Z	A
2	C	D	E	F	G	H	I	J	K	L	M	N	O	P	Q	R	S	T	U	V	W	X	Y	Z	A	B
3	D	E	F	G	H	I	J	K	L	M	N	O	P	Q	R	S	T	U	V	W	X	Y	Z	A	B	C
4	E	F	G	H	I	J	K	L	M	N	O	P	Q	R	S	T	U	V	W	X	Y	Z	A	B	C	D
5	F	G	H	I	J	K	L	M	N	O	P	Q	R	S	T	U	V	W	X	Y	Z	A	B	C	D	E
6	G	H	I	J	K	L	M	N	O	P	Q	R	S	T	U	V	W	X	Y	Z	A	B	C	D	E	F
7	H	I	J	K	L	M	N	O	P	Q	R	S	T	U	V	W	X	Y	Z	A	B	C	D	E	F	G
8	I	J	K	L	M	N	O	P	Q	R	S	T	U	V	W	X	Y	Z	A	B	C	D	E	F	G	H
9	J	K	L	M	N	O	P	Q	R	S	T	U	V	W	X	Y	Z	A	B	C	D	E	F	G	H	I
10	K	L	M	N	O	P	Q	R	S	T	U	V	W	X	Y	Z	A	B	C	D	E	F	G	H	I	J
11	L	M	N	O	P	Q	R	S	T	U	V	W	X	Y	Z	A	B	C	D	E	F	G	H	I	J	K
12	M	N	O	P	Q	R	S	T	U	V	W	X	Y	Z	A	B	C	D	E	F	G	H	I	J	K	L
13	N	O	P	Q	R	S	T	U	V	W	X	Y	Z	A	B	C	D	E	F	G	H	I	J	K	L	M
14	O	P	Q	R	S	T	U	V	W	X	Y	Z	A	B	C	D	E	F	G	H	I	J	K	L	M	N
15	P	Q	R	S	T	U	V	W	X	Y	Z	A	B	C	D	E	F	G	H	I	J	K	L	M	N	O
16	Q	R	S	T	U	V	W	X	Y	Z	A	B	C	D	E	F	G	H	I	J	K	L	M	N	O	P
17	R	S	T	U	V	W	X	Y	Z	A	B	C	D	E	F	G	H	I	J	K	L	M	N	O	P	Q
18	S	T	U	V	W	X	Y	Z	A	B	C	D	E	F	G	H	I	J	K	L	M	N	O	P	Q	R
19	T	U	V	W	X	Y	Z	A	B	C	D	E	F	G	H	I	J	K	L	M	N	O	P	Q	R	S
20	U	V	W	X	Y	Z	A	B	C	D	E	F	G	H	I	J	K	L	M	N	O	P	Q	R	S	T
21	V	W	X	Y	Z	A	B	C	D	E	F	G	H	I	J	K	L	M	N	O	P	Q	R	S	T	U
22	W	X	Y	Z	A	B	C	D	E	F	G	H	I	J	K	L	M	N	O	P	Q	R	S	T	U	V
23	X	Y	Z	A	B	C	D	E	F	G	H	I	J	K	L	M	N	O	P	Q	R	S	T	U	V	W
24	Y	Z	A	B	C	D	E	F	G	H	I	J	K	L	M	N	O	P	Q	R	S	T	U	V	W	X
25	Z	A	B	C	D	E	F	G	H	I	J	K	L	M	N	O	P	Q	R	S	T	U	V	W	X	Y

*End with ciphertext **W**, the letter where Row 3 and the column under **t** meet.*

Example: Use the Vigenère square to encrypt and decrypt.

Encrypt Key 3

plaintext:	t	i	g	e	r
CIPHERTEXT:	W	L			

Decrypt Key 3

plaintext:	l			
CIPHERTEXT:	O	L	R	Q

1. Use the Vigenère square to encrypt.

Key 5

plaintext:	w	a	s	h	i	n	g	t	o	n								
CIPHERTEXT:	B																	

2. Use the Vigenère square to decrypt the answer to the puzzle.

Riddle: What is smaller than an ant's mouth?
Answer:

Key 8

plaintext:																		
CIPHERTEXT:	E	P	I	B		B	P	M		I	V	B		M	I	B	A	

Caesar Ciphers: More Encrypting

For each problem, think of an item from the category and write it in the plaintext boxes. Choose a key, and encrypt with that key. Later, you can use your answers for a class game.

Example: Something you might put on your head

Key 7

plaintext:	f	e	d	o	r	a												
CIPHERTEXT:	M	L	K	V	Y	H												

1. Something you might put on your head

Key ____

plaintext:																		
CIPHERTEXT:																		

2. An animal that is bigger than a breadbox

Key ____

plaintext:																		
CIPHERTEXT:																		

3. A president of the United States

Key ____

plaintext:																		
CIPHERTEXT:																		

4. Something that is red

Key ____

plaintext:																		
CIPHERTEXT:																		

Caesar Ciphers: More Decrypting

Decrypt the answer to each riddle. Each has been encrypted with a Caesar cipher.

1. **Riddle:** Why can't you tell an egg a joke?
   Answer: Key 23

   F Q   J F D E Q   Z O X Z H   R M

2. **Riddle:** What do you call a snail on a ship?
   Answer: Key 13

   N   F A N V Y B E

3. **Riddle:** Why was Cinderella bad at soccer?
   Answer: Key 12

   N Q O M G E Q   E T Q   D M Z

   M I M K   R D A Y   F T Q   N M X X

4. **Riddle:** What did one eye say to the other?
   Answer: Key 18

   T W L O W W F   Q G M   S F V   E W

   K G E W L Z A F Y   K E W D D K

5. **Riddle:** What makes a road broad?
   Answer: Key 3

   W K H   O H W W H U   E

Caesar Ciphers: Cracking

Cracking means decrypting a message when you don't know the key. If you figured out the answer to the riddle on *Exploring Patterns 1* (page 3), then you have already cracked at least one message. On this page, you can crack more.

The shift pattern in a Caesar cipher can help you crack a Caesar message. You only need to guess one letter. Set your Caesar wheel so it shows how to decrypt that letter, then use the same setting to decrypt the rest of the message. Or, find the row in the Vigenère square that decrypts that letter, and use it to decrypt the rest of the message.

1. F V B V U S F U L L K V U L

   S L A A L Y A V J Y H J R H

   J H L Z H Y J P W O L Y

   Key _____ Describe your strategy.

   ____

   ____

   ____

2. K Y V J D R C C N F I U J R I V

   M V I P Y V C G W L C

   Key _____ Describe your strategy.

   ____

   ____

   ____

3. U F ' E Q M E K U R F T Q D Q

   M D Q M B A E F D A B T Q E

   Key _____ Describe your strategy.

   ____

   ____

   ____

4. W X E N V K N A 2 5 , 2 0 2 1

   R B C Q J W T B P R E R W P M J H

   Key _____ Describe your strategy.

   ____

   ____

   ____

Caesar Ciphers: More Cracking 1

Crack these messages, which were encrypted with Caesar ciphers.

1. F D F L W W J   E S P   X Z D E

   N Z X X Z Y   W P E E P C   T D   P

   Key ____ Describe your strategy.

   ____

   ____

   ____

2. A R A N U I A O O W C A X A Y K I A O

   D W N Z A N E B P D A N A W N A J K X

   N A W G O

   Key ____ Describe your strategy.

   ____

   ____

   ____

3. W X   Y A X K U N V   F Q N W

   C Q N A N   J A N

   L X W B N L D C R E N   U N C C N A B .

   Key ____ Describe your strategy.

   ____

   ____

   ____

4. H I E V   F S F ,

   G V E G O   X L M W   S R I .

   W M R G I V I P C ,

   E P M G I

   Key ____ Describe your strategy.

   ____

   ____

   ____

5. D D S E S K   D G N W   V G M T D W

   D W L L W J K

   Key ____ Describe your strategy.

   ____

   ____

   ____

Caesar Ciphers: More Cracking 2

Crack these messages. Write the key that was used to encrypt.

1. Key ______

A O Y L L   T H F   R L L W   H   Z L J Y L A   P M

A D V   V M   A O L T   H Y L   K L H K .

— I L U   M Y H U R S P U

2. Key ______

P D A N A   W N A   K J H U   P S A J P U - O E T   H A P P A N O

E J   P D A   W H L D W X A P ,   X Q P   P D A U   Y W J

N A Y K N Z   W J   E J B E J E P A   J Q I X A N   K B

E Z A W O .

3. Key ______

G W C U C A B J M D M Z G K T M D M Z . G W C K Z I K S M

L B P Q A U M A A I O M I V L Q B L W M A V ' B M D M V P

I D M I V G A X I K M A J M B E M M V E W Z L A .

Chapter 2

Additive Ciphers

Exploring Patterns 2

1. Figure out the answer to the riddle below. Use the cipher table to show how the letters were encrypted with numbers. Find a pattern to complete the cipher table.

Why did the chicken cross the playground?

t	o																							
21	16		8	6	21		21	16		21	9	6		16	21	9	6	19		20	13	10	5	6

Cipher Table

a	b	c	d	e	f	g	h	i	j	k	l	m	n	o	p	q	r	s	t	u	v	w	x	y	z
0	*1*	*2*	*3*	*4*	*5*	*6*	*7*	*8*	*9*	*10*	*11*	*12*	*13*	*14*	*15*	*16*	*17*	*18*	*19*	*20*	*21*	*22*	*23*	*24*	*25*
														16					21						

2. Use the cipher table to decrypt the message below.

21 16   6 15 4 19 0 17 21 ,   24 6   4 9 2 15 8 6 5

13 6 21 21 6 19 20   21 16   15 22 14 3 6 19 20 ,   21 9 6 15

2 5 5 6 5   21 24 16 .

Additive Ciphers: Encrypting

a	b	c	d	e	f	g	h	i	j	k	l	m	n	o	p	q	r	s	t	u	v	w	x	y	z
0	1	2	3	4	5	6	7	8	9	10	11	12	13	14	15	16	17	18	19	20	21	22	23	24	25

The last message on the previous page was encrypted with an additive cipher with key 2.

To encrypt with an **additive cipher**, first choose a number to be the **key**. Then change your message to numbers using a letter-to-number table like the one above. Finally, add the key to each number. If you get a number greater than 25 when you add, replace it with the number that matches when you wrap around a circle as shown in the figure. This way, 26 becomes 0, 27 becomes 1, and so on.

In additive ciphers, we only work with the numbers 0 to 25, since they are the numbers that match the letters.

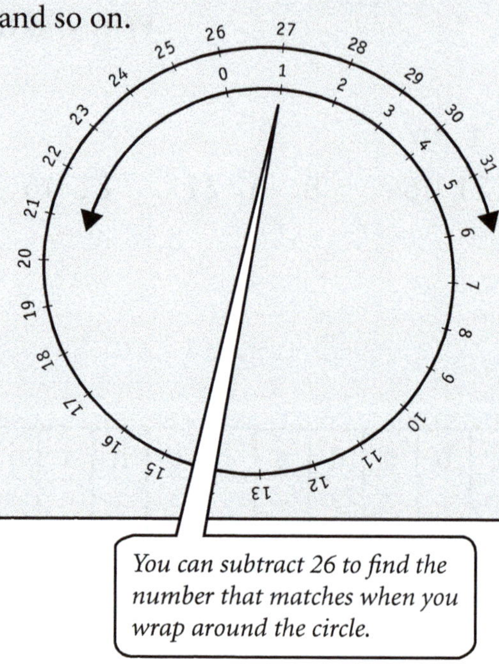

Example: Encrypt.

Key 7

plaintext:	s	i	d	e	w	a	y	s
plaintext number:	18	8	3	4	22			
CIPHERNUMBER:	25	15	10	11	~~29~~ 3			

Add 7

1. Encrypt.

Key 6

plaintext:	r	e	a	d		w	r	i	t	e		
plaintext number:												
CIPHERNUMBER:												

2. Encrypt.

Key 12

plaintext:	r	e	a	d		w	r	i	t	e		
plaintext number:												
CIPHERNUMBER:												

Replacing a number with the number between 0 and 25 that matches it when you wrap around a circle as shown above is called **reducing mod 26.**

Notation: We write **29 mod 26 = 3** to mean that 29 reduces to 3 when we wrap around a circle of size 26.

Additive Ciphers: More Encrypting

a	b	c	d	e	f	g	h	i	j	k	l	m	n	o	p	q	r	s	t	u	v	w	x	y	z
0	1	2	3	4	5	6	7	8	9	10	11	12	13	14	15	16	17	18	19	20	21	22	23	24	25

For each problem, think of an item from the category and write it in the plaintext boxes. Choose a key, and encrypt with that key. Later, you can use your answers for a class game.

Example: Something you might find in the kitchen

Key 20

plaintext:	c	a	n		o	p	e	n	e	r								
plaintext number:	2	0	13		14	15	4	13	4	17								
CIPHERNUMBER:	22	20	7 ~~33~~															

1. Something you might find in the kitchen

Key ____

plaintext:																		
plaintext number:																		
CIPHERNUMBER:																		

2. Something you will have when you grow up

Key ____

plaintext:																		
plaintext number:																		
CIPHERNUMBER:																		

3. Make up your own category: ______________________________

Key ____

plaintext:																		
plaintext number:																		
CIPHERNUMBER:																		

Additive Ciphers: Decrypting

a	b	c	d	e	f	g	h	i	j	k	l	m	n	o	p	q	r	s	t	u	v	w	x	y	z
0	1	2	3	4	5	6	7	8	9	10	11	12	13	14	15	16	17	18	19	20	21	22	23	24	25

To decrypt a message, do the opposite of what was done to encrypt it. The opposite, or inverse, of addition is subtraction. If someone added to encrypt, you can subtract to decrypt.

Example: Decrypt the answer to the riddle. It was encrypted by adding 7, so subtract 7 from each cipher number to decrypt.

Riddle: What has an eye but cannot see?

Answer:

Key 7

plaintext:	a							
plaintext number:	0							
CIPHERNUMBER:	7		20	11	11	10	18	11

Decrypt the answers to the following riddles.

1. **Riddle:** How can you make a fire with only one stick?

Answer:

Key 3

plaintext:	u															
plaintext number:	20															
CIPHERNUMBER:	23	21	7		3		15	3	22	5	10	21	22	11	5	13

2. **Riddle:** What building has the most stories?

Answer:

Key 5

plaintext:											
plaintext number:											
CIPHERNUMBER:	24	12	9		16	13	6	22	5	22	3

Additive Ciphers: Decrypting

What Happens When You Get Negative Numbers?

a	b	c	d	e	f	g	h	i	j	k	l	m	n	o	p	q	r	s	t	u	v	w	x	y	z
0	1	2	3	4	5	6	7	8	9	10	11	12	13	14	15	16	17	18	19	20	21	22	23	24	25

To decrypt the additive ciphers on the last page, you subtracted the key and matched each number with a letter. But the table does not show how to match negative numbers with letters. What should you do if you get a negative number?

If you get a negative number when you subtract, think of the number line wrapping around a circle as shown in the figure. Replace a negative number with the number between 0 and 25 that it matches. This way, -1 becomes 25, -2 becomes 24, and so on.

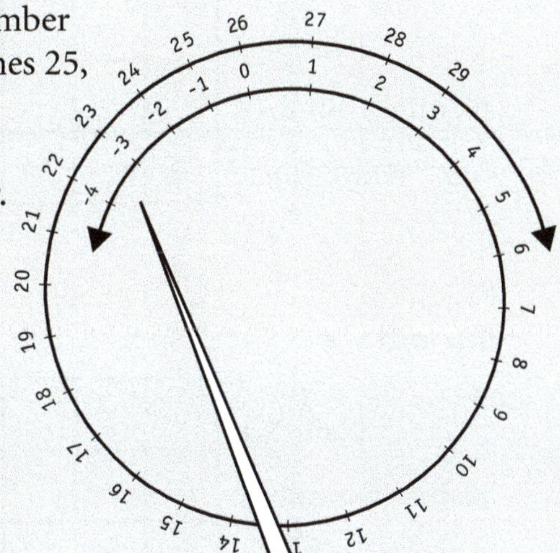

If a number is less than 0, you can add 26 to find the number that matches when you wrap around the circle.

Example: Decrypt. The key is 6, so subtract 6 from each ciphernumber.

Key 6

plaintext:	a	n	y			
plaintext number:	0	13	24 ~~-2~~			
CIPHERNUMBER:	6	19	4	2	6	4

1. Decrypt by subtracting the key. Replace negative numbers with matching numbers between 0 and 25.

A. Key 3

plaintext:	p				
plaintext number:					
CIPHERNUMBER:	18	11	2	2	3

B. Key 10

plaintext:	t			
plaintext number:				
CIPHERNUMBER:	3	10	7	18

2. **Riddle:** What do you call two people who practice medicine?

Answer:

Key 15

plaintext:													
plaintext number:													
CIPHERNUMBER:	4	15	23	6	-	15	-	1	19	18	23	17	7

Additive Ciphers: More Decrypting 1

a	b	c	d	e	f	g	h	i	j	k	l	m	n	o	p	q	r	s	t	u	v	w	x	y	z
0	1	2	3	4	5	6	7	8	9	10	11	12	13	14	15	16	17	18	19	20	21	22	23	24	25

Decrypt the answer to each riddle. Each has been encrypted with an additive cipher.

1. **Riddle:** What grows down when it grows up?
   Answer:

Key 8

plaintext:							
plaintext number:							
CIPHERNUMBER:	08		14	22	22	0	12

2. **Riddle:** What city has no people?
   Answer:

Key 10

plaintext:											
plaintext number:											
CIPHERNUMBER:	14	21	14	12	3	1	18	12	18	3	8

3. **Riddle:** What do you call a duck that gets all A's in school?
   Answer: Encrypted with key 21.

21   17 03 13 25   11 15 21 23 05 25 12

To avoid confusion when we write numbers without a grid, we put 0 in front of one-digit numbers.

4. **Riddle:** What goes up a chimney down but won't go down a chimney up?
   Answer: Encrypted with key 15.

15 02   09 01 16 06 19 00 00 15

Additive Ciphers: Decrypting
Making Calculations Simpler

a	b	c	d	e	f	g	h	i	j	k	l	m	n	o	p	q	r	s	t	u	v	w	x	y	z
0	1	2	3	4	5	6	7	8	9	10	11	12	13	14	15	16	17	18	19	20	21	22	23	24	25

There are several ways to decrypt an additive cipher. Which one makes your calculations simpler depends on the situation.

Example: Decrypt.

Key 20

plaintext:	t				
plaintext number:	19 ~~-7~~				
CIPHERNUMBER:	13	2	0	24	11

Method 1. Subtract the key. If you get a negative number, add 26. This is the method you did on the last page. The work in the grid shows how to decrypt 13 this way: subtract 20 from 13 to get -7, then add 26 to reduce. You can see this in the equation:

$$\underbrace{13 - 20}_{-7} + 26 = 19$$

Method 2. Add 26 before you subtract the key. Adding 26 gives the equivalent number on the circle. In this example, we could add 13 + 26 to get 39, and then subtract 20, which is the key.

$$\underbrace{13 + 26}_{39} - 20 = 19$$

Method 3. Compute (26-key) and add that amount, since that is the same as adding 26 and then subtracting the key. In this example, first compute 26 – 20 = 6, then add 6 to 13.

$$13 + \underbrace{26 - 20}_{6} = 19$$

The equations show the same numbers are being added or subtracted, just in a different order.

Finish decrypting the example. Try using Methods 2 and 3.

1. Decrypt. Use Method 2 when needed to avoid negative numbers .

Key 20

t									
19 ~~39~~									
13	8	9		12	24	22	11	24	13

2. Use Method 3 to decrypt. To decrypt with key 10, you can subtract ____ or add ____.

Key 10

11	4	1	18	14	13		3	1	14	10	2	4	1	14	2

Additive Ciphers: More Decrypting 2

a	b	c	d	e	f	g	h	i	j	k	l	m	n	o	p	q	r	s	t	u	v	w	x	y	z
0	1	2	3	4	5	6	7	8	9	10	11	12	13	14	15	16	17	18	19	20	21	22	23	24	25

Decrypt the answer to each riddle. Each has been encrypted with an additive cipher.

1. **Riddle:** What did the strawberry say to the blueberry?
   Answer: Encrypted with key 12, so decrypt by subtracting _____ or adding _____.

   08 19 10 04 00 13 23 06 16 ?

2. **Riddle:** How was the Roman Empire cut in half?
   Answer: Encrypted with key 21, so decrypt by subtracting _____ or adding _____.

   17 03 14 02 21 10 21 03 12 09 00 23 21 25 13 21 12 13

3. **Riddle:** What is out of bounds?
   Answer: Encrypted with key 10, so decrypt by subtracting _____ or adding _____.

   10 23 14 07 17 10 04 02 03 14 13 20 10 23 16 10 01 24 24

4. **Riddle:** Why do birds fly south in the winter?
   Answer: Encrypted with key 25, so decrypt by subtracting _____ or adding _____.

   18 13 13 04 25 16 18 13 21 25 10 09

Additive Ciphers: Cracking

a	b	c	d	e	f	g	h	i	j	k	l	m	n	o	p	q	r	s	t	u	v	w	x	y	z
0	1	2	3	4	5	6	7	8	9	10	11	12	13	14	15	16	17	18	19	20	21	22	23	24	25

Each messge below was encrypted with an additive cipher. Crack each one, and describe what clues in the message helped you to crack it. Write the key that was added to encrypt. *Hint: What could one-letter words be? What could consecutive numbers be? What numbers occur most often?*

1. 21 09 19 13   09

   12 17 14 14 13 00 13 22 11 13

   — 01 03 10 02 00 09 11 02

   Key _____ Describe your strategy.

   ____

   ____

   ____

2. 05 19 16   17 20 03 04 05

   05 19 03 16 16   15 20 18 20 05 04

   00 17   01 20   12 03 16

   05 19 03 16 16   00 25 16

   17 00 06 03 .

   Key _____ Describe your strategy.

   ____

   ____

   ____

3. 16 17 18 21 00 21 06 17 24 11 19

   01 01 16 06 01 07 05 17 00 07 25

   14 17 04 05 18 01 04 05 17 15 04

   17 06 25 17 05 05 13 19 17 05

   Key _____ Describe your strategy.

   ____

   ____

   ____

Additive Ciphers: More Cracking 1

a	b	c	d	e	f	g	h	i	j	k	l	m	n	o	p	q	r	s	t	u	v	w	x	y	z
0	1	2	3	4	5	6	7	8	9	10	11	12	13	14	15	16	17	18	19	20	21	22	23	24	25

Each message was encrypted with an additive cipher. Crack and decrypt each message.

Message 1: Key _______

11 18 10 25 02 15 16 24 15 02 17 05 02 10 24 16 17 02 15 16

12 03 17 05 02 20 02 24 08 , 25 18 17 17 05 02

16 09 24 19 02 16 12 03 17 05 02 16 17 15 12 11 04 .

— 00 05 24 15 09 02 16 25 24 25 25 24 04 02

Message 2: Key _______

01 12 09 18 03 19 25 12 05 00 09 17 05 23 24 09 22 09 08

18 25 17 06 09 22 23 , 03 19 25 01 13 16 16 13 18 10 05 07 24

18 19 16 19 18 11 09 22 06 09 22 09 05 08 13 18 11

18 25 17 06 09 22 23 , 05 18 05 17 19 22 09 24 12 05 18 03 19 25

22 09 05 08 01 19 22 08 23 01 12 09 18 22 09 05 08 13 18 11

06 19 19 15 23 . 03 19 25 01 13 16 16 06 09 22 09 05 08 13 18 11

17 09 05 18 13 18 11 23 . — 01 . 09 . 06 . 08 25 06 19 13 23

Additive Ciphers: More Cracking 2

a	b	c	d	e	f	g	h	i	j	k	l	m	n	o	p	q	r	s	t	u	v	w	x	y	z
0	1	2	3	4	5	6	7	8	9	10	11	12	13	14	15	16	17	18	19	20	21	22	23	24	25

Each animal name has been encrypted using an additive cipher. Match the animal to the encrypted word. Identify the key in each case. One has been done for you.

1. e e l *4 4 11*	A. 04 03 22	key____	
2. c a t	B. 11 16 11	key____	
3. b a t	C. 09 07 00	key____	
4. p u p	D. 24 24 05	key *20*	(since 4 + 20 = 24)

5. l y n x	E. 25 14 00 15	key____
6. l a m b	F. 14 01 16 00	key____
7. b o a r	G. 10 23 09 00	key____
8. b e a r	H. 15 18 14 05	key____

9. h o r s e	I. 17 19 19 23 09	key____
10. m o o s e	J. 02 09 12 13 25	key____
11. c a m e l	K. 02 20 04 23 20	key____
12. s k u n k	L. 10 08 20 12 19	key____

Chapter 3

Keyword and Other Substitution Ciphers

Exploring Patterns 3

The message below was encrypted with a keyword cipher, which is different from a Caesar cipher, so a cipher wheel won't help you crack it.

1. Some of the letters in the message have been decrypted for you. Crack the rest of the message and record substitutions in the table as you go. Look for a pattern and complete the table.

   TIP: Once you know one substitution, make the same subsititution throughout the message. It will help you see others.

a	b	c	d	e	f	g	h	i	j	k	l	m	n	o	p	q	r	s	t	u	v	w	x	y	z
		T	I	M			B	C		F				K	L		O					U		W	

k e y w o r d   c i p h e r

Y F M W U K O I T C L B M O C P Y Q W L M K E

P R Z P Q C Q R Q C K J T C L B M O Q B Y Q R P M P

Y F M W U K O I Y J I F M W G M Q Q M O Q K H Y F M

C Q P T C L B M O Q Y Z G M . T Y J W K R A R M P P

U B Y Q Q B M W Y O M C J Q B M Q Y Z G M Y Z K S M ?

2. The cipher table was built with a special word, the keyword, and a special letter, the keyletter. Can you see what they are?

   Keyword: ____________________ Keyletter: __________

Keyword Ciphers: Encrypting and Decrypting

A **keyword cipher** is a type of substitution cipher. To make the cipher table for a keyword cipher, first choose a **keyword** and a **keyletter**. Then write the keyword under the alphabet, starting under the keyletter. If a letter appears more than once in the keyword, write it only the first time it appears. Continue with the unused letters in alphabetical order, wrapping around until the table is filled.

Example: Here is the cipher table for a keyword cipher.

Keyword **APPLE**, Keyletter **g**

a	b	c	d	e	f	g	h	i	j	k	l	m	n	o	p	q	r	s	t	u	v	w	x	y	z
U	V	W	X	Y	Z	A	P	L	E	B	C	D	F	G	H	I	J	K	M	N	O	Q	R	S	T

*Start the keyword **APPLE** under the keyletter **g**. Leave out the second **P** in **APPLE**.*

*Write the unused letters in alphabetical order. The letter **A** has already been used, so start with **B**.*

Use the table to encrypt and decrypt.

A. Encrypt

plaintext:	p	e	a	r
CIPHERTEXT:	H			

B. Decrypt

plaintext:	b					
CIPHERTEXT:	V	U	F	U	F	U

Complete the cipher tables for the keyword ciphers below. Then decrypt.

1.

Keyword **HORSE**, Keyletter **m**

a	b	c	d	e	f	g	h	i	j	k	l	m	n	o	p	q	r	s	t	u	v	w	x	y	z

Riddle: What kind of horses go out after dark?

Answer:

O	W	U	V	C	H	L	A	Q	B

2.

Keyword **MISSISSIPPI**, Keyletter **d**

a	b	c	d	e	f	g	h	i	j	k	l	m	n	o	p	q	r	s	t	u	v	w	x	y	z

Riddle: Two flies are on the porch. Which one is the actor?

Answer:

O	A	I		H	G	I		H	G		O	A	I		N	Z	L	I	I	G

Keyword Ciphers: More Encrypting

For each problem, think of an item from the category and write it in the plaintext boxes. Pick a keyword and a keyletter and encrypt. Use a different keyword for each category. Later, you can use your answers for a class game.

1. Something you should not eat before dinner

Keyword ______________________ Keyletter ____

a	b	c	d	e	f	g	h	i	j	k	l	m	n	o	p	q	r	s	t	u	v	w	x	y	z

plaintext:																						
CIPHERTEXT:																						

2. A good book to read

Keyword ______________________ Keyletter ____

a	b	c	d	e	f	g	h	i	j	k	l	m	n	o	p	q	r	s	t	u	v	w	x	y	z

plaintext:																						
CIPHERTEXT:																						

3. Something that is purple

Keyword ______________________ Keyletter ____

a	b	c	d	e	f	g	h	i	j	k	l	m	n	o	p	q	r	s	t	u	v	w	x	y	z

plaintext:																						
CIPHERTEXT:																						

Keyword Ciphers: More Decrypting

For each problem, make a cipher table with the given keyword and keyletter. Then, decrypt the message.

1. Keyword **PROVERB** Keyletter **m**

a	b	c	d	e	f	g	h	i	j	k	l	m	n	o	p	q	r	s	t	u	v	w	x	y	z

Q F Q R   P O R Y Q I A   P K I   S K Z Z   S B O P   C B Q Q A .

— Korean proverb

2. Keyword **ALABAMA** Keyletter **k**

a	b	c	d	e	f	g	h	i	j	k	l	m	n	o	p	q	r	s	t	u	v	w	x	y	z

T U K   A M C H   H F I G G U T   O C F U   G D U L L

S X U E I U F .

3. Keyword **NAPOLEON** Keyletter **q**

a	b	c	d	e	f	g	h	i	j	k	l	m	n	o	p	q	r	s	t	u	v	w	x	y	z

X K E K A   S X O K A A L Z O   D Y L A   K X K W D   B R K X

R K   S P   W G U S X Q   G   W S P O G U K .

— Napoleon Bonaparte

Keyword Ciphers: Cracking

A keyword cipher is harder to crack than a Caesar cipher because the pattern in its cipher table is more complicated. But, since it is a type of substitution cipher, letter frequencies can help. The keyword pattern in the cipher table can help too.

1. Use the frequency table to record the number of times each letter occurs in the message.
2. Use your data to help crack the message. A good first guess is that the most common letters in the message match the most common letters in English, which are **e**, **t**, **a**, **o**, and **i**. But don't expect the common letters to match exactly.
3. Fill in the cipher table as you go along. Look for the keyword to emerge in the bottom row.

a	b	c	d	e	f	g	h	i	j	k	l	m	n	o	p	q	r	s	t	u	v	w	x	y	z

KEYWORD ________________ Keyletter ______

N IUPY U XJYUC MIUM EDY

XUS MINL DUMNED QNBB

JNLY OF UDX BNPY EOM

MIY MJOY CYUDNDK EZ NML

WJYYX: "QY IEBX MIYLY

MJOMIL ME VY LYBZ-

YPNXYDM: MIUM UBB CYD

UJY WJYUMYX YHOUB."

Frequency Table

Letter	Tallies	Number
A		
B		
C		
D		
E		
F		
G		
H		
I		
J		
K		
L		
M		
N		
O		
P		
Q		
R		
S		
T		
U		
V		
W		
X		
Y		
Z		

Keyword Ciphers: More Cracking

Find the frequencies of the letters in the following message and use them to crack the message. Fill in the cipher table as you go along, and look for a keyword cipher pattern to emerge.

a	b	c	d	e	f	g	h	i	j	k	l	m	n	o	p	q	r	s	t	u	v	w	x	y	z

KEYWORD ________________ Keyletter ______

Q WKTKC NIKAA. QP QA F

HFYQPFU VQAPFSK PX

POKXCQEK GKMXCK XWK OFA

JFPF. QWAKWAQGUD XWK

GKNQWA PX PLQAP MFHPA

PX AIQP POKXCQKA,

QWAPKFJ XM POKXCQKA PX

AIQP MFHPA.

—AOKCUXHS OXUVKA

Frequency Table

Letter	Tallies	Number
A		
B		
C		
D		
E		
F		
G		
H		
I		
J		
K		
L		
M		
N		
O		
P		
Q		
R		
S		
T		
U		
V		
W		
X		
Y		
Z		

Letter Frequencies: Definitions

On the next page, you will examine sample English text to find the most and least common letters. This page discusses the terms "frequency" and "relative frequency," which are often used to describe how common something is.

The **frequency** of a letter in a message is the number of times it occurs. The **relative frequency** is a ratio that compares or relates the number of occurrences of the letter to the total number of letters. It tells how common a letter is in a message.

$$\text{relative frequency} = \frac{\text{number of occurences}}{\text{total number of letters}}$$

You can express the relative frequency as a fraction, decimal, or percent.

Example 1: The frequency of **s** in **miss** is 2, since **s** occurs two times. The relative frequency of **s** in **miss** is 2/4 or 1/2, since the total number of letters is 4. It can also be expressed as 0.50 or 50%.

Example 2: The frequency of **s** in **insects** is also 2. The relative frequency of **s** in **insects** is 2/7 . You can use a calculator to change 2/7 to a decimal:

$$2/7 = 2 \div 7$$
$$\approx .285714286 \text{ (as shown on a calculator)}$$
$$\approx 0.286 \text{ (rounded to three decimal places)}$$

To change 0.286 to percent, multiply by 100 and get 28.6%.

Even though the frequency of **s** in both **miss** and **insects** is the same, the relative frequencies are different. Because 28.6% < 50%, we say that the **s** in **insects** is less common than the **s** in **miss**.

---

1. Consider the following message:

`W h e r e   t h e r e ' s   a   w i l l   t h e r e ' s   a   w a y .`

A. Find the total number of letters in the message. __________

B. Complete the table to show the frequency and relative frequency of **a, e,** and **t** in the message.

Letter	Frequency	Relative Frequency		
		Fraction	Decimal (to 3 places)	Percent
a				
e				
t				

Letter Frequencies: Examining English Text

If you analyzed a very long message, you would most likely find that **e**, **t**, **a**, **o**, and **i** are the most common letters, in that order. Table 1 shows frequencies of letters in English computed from a sample of about 100,000 letters. On this page, you will examine a sample of about 100 letters to explore whether samples of that size have frequencies similar to those in Table 1.

Table 1. * Frequency in English text

Letter	%
a	8.2
b	1.5
c	2.8
d	4.3
e	12.7
f	2.2
g	2.0
h	6.1
i	7.0
j	0.2
k	0.8
l	4.0
m	2.4
n	6.7
o	7.5
p	1.9
q	0.1
r	6.0
s	6.3
t	9.1
u	2.8
v	1.0
w	2.4
x	0.1
y	2.0
z	0.1

Table 2. Frequencies in Sample

Letter	Tallies	Number	Rel. Freq. %
a			
b			
c			
d			
e			
f			
g			
h			
i			
j			
k			
l			
m			
n			
o			
p			
q			
r			
s			
t			
u			
v			
w			
x			
y			
z			
	total		

1. Choose about three lines from the article on the next page, or pick a sample of text from some other English source.

2. Use Table 2 to record the number of occurences of each letter in your text. Then compute the relative frequencies.

3. Highlight the five most common letters in Table 2. Are they the same as in Table 1?

____

4. Complete the list of the five most common letters in Table 1. Then list your top five from Table 2. Put them in order from most to least.

Top 5 in Table 1

e	12.7

Top 5 in Table 2

5. How do your most common and least common letters compare with those in Table 1?

____

____

____

6. What do you think would happen if you picked a different sample of letters?

____

____

____

* from H. Beker and F. Piper. Cipher Systems: The Protection of Communications. Northwood Publications, London, 1982

Letter Frequencies: Sample English Text

Choose about three lines from the article. Find the frequency of letters in your sample, using Table 2 on the previous page to record your data.

Substitutions Ciphers and Mary Queen of Scots

The substitution ciphers we've seen so far—the Caesar, additive, and keyword ciphers—all have patterns in their cipher tables. It usually isn't too hard to crack these ciphers because, after you guess a few letters, the patterns in their cipher tables help you figure out the key and complete the table. You might think that, if you make a substitution cipher that doesn't have any obvious pattern in its table, it would be very difficult or impossible to crack. After all, there are 26 x 25 x 24 x . . . x 2 x 1 = 403,291,4 61,126,605,635,584,000,000 possible ways to fill in a cipher table, so how could someone guess which way you used to make your cipher? If they guess a new way every minute, it would take them about 767 quintillion years (that's a billion billion) to try them all. But you don't have to try every possible substitution table to crack a substitution cipher. Letter frequencies and patterns in the English language can make cracking much easier than that.

In 1586, Mary Queen of Scots learned the hard way that substitution ciphers can be cracked. Mary was the Catholic Queen of Scotland and her cousin Elizabeth was the Protestant Queen of England. When Mary came to England to escape problems in Scotland, Elizabeth worried that she would try to become Queen of England. So Elizabeth imprisoned Mary in a castle, where she remained for 18 years. During that time, Catholics loyal to Mary developed a plot to assassinate Elizabeth and cause a rebellion that would lead to Mary taking over the throne. They sent messages back and forth to Mary describing their plot. They encrypted the messages to keep them secret, but they made a big mistake: they used a cipher that wasn't strong enough. It was similar to a substitution cipher and it could be cracked with frequency analysis. Elizabeth's spies stole the messages and cracked them, revealing Mary's plot. Then, they pretended to be Mary and sent a message that asked for the names of the other people involved in the plot. They encrypted the message with Mary's cipher, so Mary's friends would think it was from her. This tricked her friends into revealing the names of the others involved in the plot. Consequently, every one of the conspirators was arrested.

Elizabeth's advisors had been trying to convince her that Mary was plotting against her, but they didn't have enough proof. These encrypted messages, once they were cracked, provided the proof needed to convince her. Elizabeth then agreed to have her cousin Mary executed.

Substitution Ciphers: Make Your Own Table

A **simple substitution cipher** replaces each letter of the alphabet with another letter. The ciphers we have studied so far are all examples of simple substitution ciphers. They each have special patterns in their cipher tables, but not all substitution ciphers have patterns. The letters could be scrambled up in any order. Here is a cipher table for a substitution cipher that has no obvious pattern.

Example:

A sample substitution cipher table

a	b	c	d	e	f	g	h	i	j	k	l	m	n	o	p	q	r	s	t	u	v	w	x	y	z
D	X	M	E	Z	W	V	H	L	A	N	K	G	O	B	U	P	T	J	F	C	S	Q	I	Y	R

Decrypting: Decrypt the message using this table

plaintext:																		
CIPHERTEXT:	M	L	U	H	Z	T		F	D	X	K	Z						

1. Make your own substitution cipher by entering cipher letters into the second row of the cipher table.

Name of cipher: ____________________

a	b	c	d	e	f	g	h	i	j	k	l	m	n	o	p	q	r	s	t	u	v	w	x	y	z

2. For each problem, think of an item from the category and write it in the plaintext boxes. Encrypt using your cipher. Later, classmates can decrypt your messages.

A. Something you use in CryptoClub

plaintext:																						
CIPHERTEXT:																						

B. Something you use in math class

plaintext:																						
CIPHERTEXT:																						

Substitution Ciphers: Make Your Own Pattern

If you encrypt a message with a substitution cipher that has no patterns, you will have to provide the whole cipher table if you want a friend to decrypt your message. However, if you use a pattern, you could just say the pattern, and then your friend could recreate the table. Did you use a pattern for your ciphers on page 36?

1. Make your own substitution cipher by entering cipher letters into the second row of the cipher table. Think of a way to fill in the table that uses a pattern. Do not use a shift pattern or a keyword pattern; make up something new.

Name of cipher: ____________________

a	b	c	d	e	f	g	h	i	j	k	l	m	n	o	p	q	r	s	t	u	v	w	x	y	z

2. Describe the pattern you used so that others can recreate the table from your description.

____

____

____

____

3. Think of something from one of the categories on page 36. Enter it in the plaintext boxes, then encrypt using your cipher.

plaintext:																						
CIPHERTEXT:																						

4. Share your pattern with the class and challenge them to decrypt your message.

There are more cipher tables on page 81 to make more substitution cipher tables using different patterns.

Substitution Ciphers: Cracking

Using Letter Frequencies

The message below is encrypted with a substitution cipher that has no special pattern in its cipher table. The relative frequencies of the letters in the message are given. Compare them with the frequencies of letters in English to help guess the correct substitutions to crack the message. Record your substitutions in the cipher table.

H OHVDJBV SHDM VN VIJ

MNRVNP, "DV IEPVS

XIJPJYJP D VNERI. DV

DS OHDBCEK VN VNERI

LZ SINEKMJP, LZ ABJJ,

HBM LZ IJHM." "NI,"

PJOKDJM VIJ MNRVNP,

"D ABNX VIJ OPNUKJL

—ZNE IHYJ H UPNAJB

CDBQJP!"

Frequencies

In message		In English	
Letter	%	Letter	%
J	12.1	e	12.7
N	10	t	9.1
V	10	a	8.2
I	7.9	o	7.5
D	7.1	i	7.0
P	7.1	n	6.7
H	5.7	s	6.3
B	5.0	h	6.1
M	5.0	r	6.0
E	4.3	d	4.3
K	2.9	l	4.0
L	2.9	c	2.8
O	2.9	u	2.8
R	2.9	m	2.4
S	2.9	w	2.4
Z	2.9	f	2.2
A	2.1	g	2.0
C	1.4	y	2.0
U	1.4	p	1.9
X	1.4	b	1.5
Y	1.4	v	1.0
Q	0.7	k	0.8
F	0	j	0.2
G	0	q	0.1
T	0	x	0.1
W	0	z	0.1

a	b	c	d	e	f	g	h	i	j	k	l	m	n	o	p	q	r	s	t	u	v	w	x	y	z

Chapter 4

Multiplicative Ciphers

Exploring Patterns 4

1. The seven words below were encrypted with the same cipher. Figure out the words and use the cipher table to show how the letters were encrypted. Find a pattern to complete the table.

						d	*a*	*y*
14	12	9	13	12	2	9	0	20

10	16	13	9	0	20

5	21	8	25	2	9	0	20

5	8	12	2	9	0	20

2	8	13	9	0	20

15	25	24	9	0	20

2	0	5	8	25	9	0	20

Cipher Table

a	b	c	d	e	f	g	h	i	j	k	l	m	n	o	p	q	r	s	t	u	v	w	x	y	z
0	*1*	*2*	*3*	*4*	*5*	*6*	*7*	*8*	*9*	*10*	*11*	*12*	*13*	*14*	*15*	*16*	*17*	*18*	*19*	*20*	*21*	*22*	*23*	*24*	*25*
0			9																					20	

2. Use the cipher table to decrypt the following message:

05 21 24 02   05 00 03 07 12   21 00 02   00   19 00 05 05 12 25 13

07 12 15 05   05 16   25 24 18 21 05   00 13 09

00 13 16 05 21 12 25   05 16 19   05 16   03 16 05 05 16 10 .

Multiplicative Ciphers: Encrypting

a	b	c	d	e	f	g	h	i	j	k	l	m	n	o	p	q	r	s	t	u	v	w	x	y	z
0	1	2	3	4	5	6	7	8	9	10	11	12	13	14	15	16	17	18	19	20	21	22	23	24	25

The cipher used on the previous page was a multiplicative cipher with key 3. Multiplicative ciphers work just like additive ciphers except that you multiply instead of add. To encrypt with a **multiplicative cipher**, first choose a number to be the **key**. Then change your message to numbers and multiply each number by the key. If you get a number greater than 25 after you multiply, then replace it with the number you get when you wrap around the circle. You can leave your answer in numbers or change it back to letters.

Example: Encrypt the following using the multiplicative cipher with key 3.

Key 3

plaintext:	d	e	c	e	m	b	e	r
plaintext number:	3				12			
CIPHERNUMBERS:	9				10 ~~36~~			
CIPHERTEXT: (optional)	J				K			

plaintext number × key

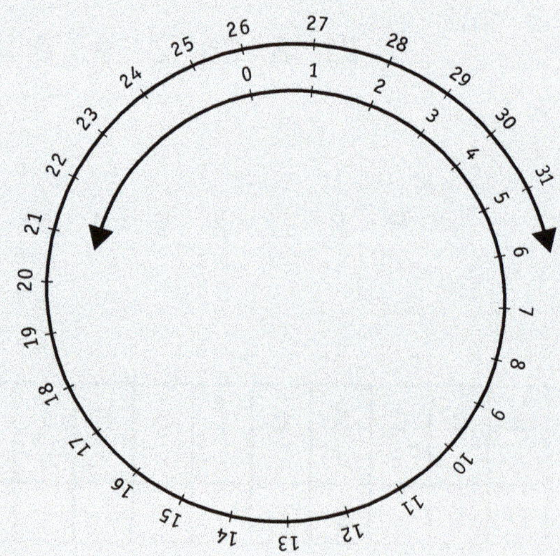

Encrypt each of the following using the multiplicative key given.

1. Key 3

plaintext:	o	c	t	o	b	e	r
plaintext number:							
CIPHERNUMBERS:							
CIPHERTEXT:							

2. Key 5

m	a	y

Reducing Mod 26: Larger Numbers

In cryptography, we use numbers between 0 and 25. If we get larger numbers, we wrap around the spiral and replace them with matching numbers between 0 and 25, as you did with additive ciphers. This is called **reducing mod 26**. With multiplicative ciphers, you will work with larger numbers than with additive ciphers. This page and the next explore how to reduce larger numbers.

Numbers that wrap around to the same position on the spiral are said to be **equivalent mod 26**. For example, 56 and 30 are equivalent mod 26.

> ***Notation:***
> *The symbol "≡" means "is equivalent to." For example,*
> *56 ≡ 30 (mod 26).*
>
> *The number 56 is equivalent to all the numbers in the same wedge of the spiral, but it reduces to only one number, the number 4.*
>
> *To show that 56 reduces to 4, we can use the ordinary equal sign, without parentheses:*
> *56 mod 26 = 4.*

Mod 26 Spiral

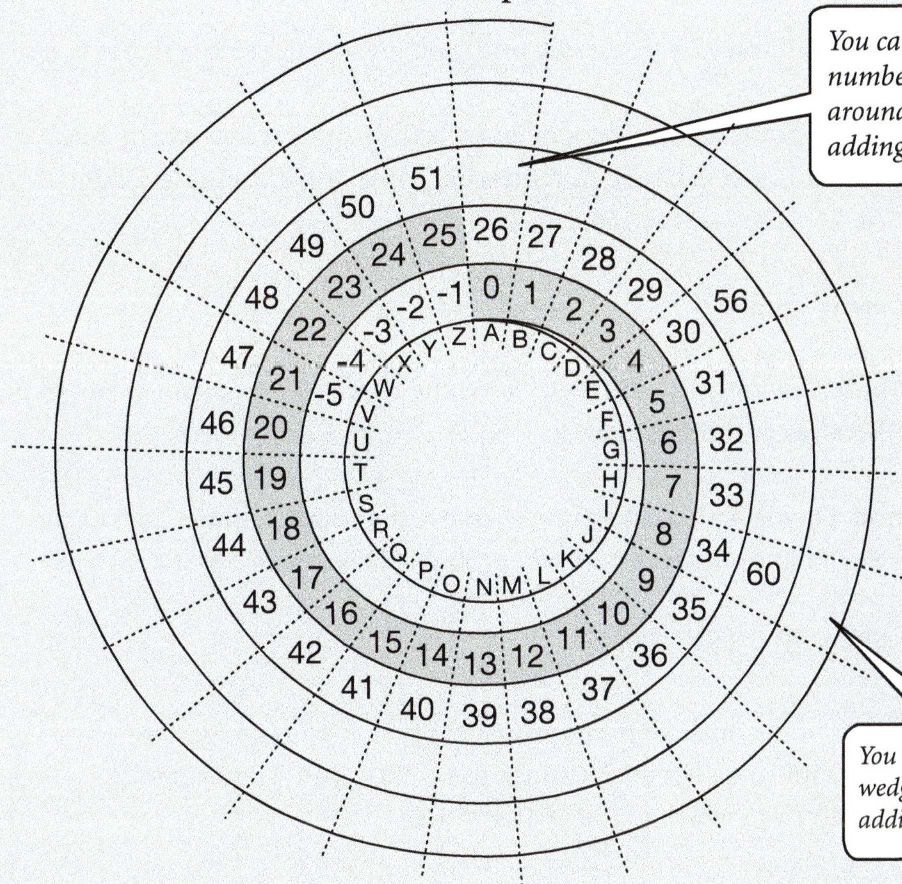

You can fill in the numbers by going around the spiral, adding one each step.

You can fill in each wedge by going out, adding 26 each step.

1. List four numbers that are equivalent to 5. ____________________

2. Reduce each number mod 26. Add missing numbers to the spiral as needed:

   A. 30 mod 26 = _______   B. 45 mod 26 = _______   C. 75 mod 26 = _______

3. Reduce these numbers that are not shown on the spiral:

   A. 120 mod 26 = __________   B. 497 mod 26 = __________

Reducing Mod 26: Finding Remainders

You don't actually have to wrap the numbers or look at the spiral to reduce a number mod 26—all you have to do is find a remainder. For example, the numbers 4, 30, and 56 each reduce to 4 (mod 26). Note that 4 is the remainder when you divide each number by 26.

Example: Reduce 120 mod 26 by finding the remainder of 120 ÷ 26. Below are several solutions. Some use substraction. Others use division.

Solutions that use subtraction:

Abby's Method. Subtract 26 repeatedly until you get an answer less than 26.

Danny's Method. Subtract multiples of 26 instead of subtracting one by one. Danny subtracted 104. It is handy to remember some of the multiples of 26:

26, 52, 78, 104, 130, 156, … , 260, …

Abby's Work

120
-26
94
-26
68
-26
42
-26
16

Danny's Work

120
-104
16

Solutions that use division:

Peter's Method. Use long division. Peter used the regular long division algorithm, and wrote "R 16" as part of his answer.

Peter's Work

$$\begin{array}{r} 4 \text{ R } 16 \\ 26\overline{)120} \\ \underline{104} \\ 16 \end{array}$$

Tim's Method. Divide with a calculator, then use the whole number part of the answer. On a calculator, your answer will probably be expressed as a decimal:

120 ÷ 26 = 4.615384615

The 4 to the left of the decimal point in 4.615384615 tells us 26 "goes into" 120 four times with some left over. Compute $4 \times 26 = 104$. The remainder is the amount left over, which is $120 - 104 = 16$.

Tim's Work

$4 \times 26 = 104$

$120 - 104 = 16$

Jenny's Method. Divide with a calculator, then use the decimal part of the answer. To get the decimal part, subtract 4 from the number 4.615384615 already in your calculator window. This gives 0.615384615. Recall that since the divisor is 26, the decimal remainder is related to the whole number remainder R by the equation:

Jenny's Work

4.615384615 – 4 = 0.615384615

0.615384615 x 26 = 16

$$\frac{R}{26} = 0.615384615\ldots \text{To find } R \text{, multiply both sides by 26: } R = 26 \times 0.615384615\ldots = 16.$$

1. Try some of the methods above to reduce each number:

A. 118 mod 26 = _____ B. 152 mod 26 = _____ C. 527 mod 26 _____ D. 2000 mod 26 = _____

Multiplicative Ciphers: More Encrypting

a	b	c	d	e	f	g	h	i	j	k	l	m	n	o	p	q	r	s	t	u	v	w	x	y	z
0	1	2	3	4	5	6	7	8	9	10	11	12	13	14	15	16	17	18	19	20	21	22	23	24	25

For each problem, think of an item from the category and write it in the plaintext boxes. Encrypt using the given multiplicative key. Convert to letters if you like. Later, you can use your answers for a class game.

Example: Something you shouldn't bring to school

Key 7

plaintext:	c	o	t	t	o	n		c	a	n	d	y
plaintext number:	2	14	19	19	14	13		2	0	13	3	24
CIPHERNUMBERS:	14	20 ~~98~~	3 ~~133~~	3								
CIPHERTEXT: (optional)	O	U	D	D								

1. Something you shouldn't bring to school

Key 5

plaintext:																		
plaintext number:																		
CIPHERNUMBERS:																		
CIPHERTEXT: (optional)																		

2. A good name for a pet fish

Key 7

plaintext:																		
plaintext number:																		
CIPHERNUMBERS:																		
CIPHERTEXT: (optional)																		

Multiplicative Ciphers: Decrypting

Using Tables

If you know that a message was encrypted with a multiplicative cipher and you know the key, you can decrypt by making a cipher table.

Example: Complete the table for the multiplicative cipher with key 5. Use it to decrypt the messages.

Times 5 Cipher Table

plaintext:	a	b	c	d	e	f	g	h	i	j	k	l	m	n	o	p	q	r	s	t	u	v	w	x	y	z
plaintext number:	0	1	2	3	4	5	6	7	8	9	10	11	12	13	14	15	16	17	18	19	20	21	22	23	24	25
CIPHERNUMBERS:	0	5	10	15	20	25	4	9	14	19	24															
CIPHERTEXT: (optional)	A	F	K	P	U	Z	E	J	O	T	Y															

Key 5

plaintext:	s					
CIPHERTEXT:	M	S	K	K	U	H

Key 5

plaintext:	f							
CIPHERNUMBER:	25	18	18	17	5	0	3	3

1. Complete the table for the multiplicative cipher with key 7.

Times 7 Cipher Table

a	b	c	d	e	f	g	h	i	j	k	l	m	n	o	p	q	r	s	t	u	v	w	x	y	z
0	1	2	3	4	5	6	7	8	9	10	11	12	13	14	15	16	17	18	19	20	21	22	23	24	25
0	7																								
A	H																								

2. Use the times 7 cipher table to decrypt the answer to the following riddle:

Riddle: When is a door not a door?
Answer Encrypted with key 7:

Y X C N   E D ' W   A   L A P

3. Use the times 3 cipher table on page 41 to decrypt the answer to the following riddle:

Riddle: What has four wheels and flies?
Answer Encrypted with key 3:

00   18 00 25 03 00 18 12   05 25 08 06 04

Multiplicative Ciphers: Good and Bad Keys

Some numbers do not make good keys for multiplicative ciphers. You can see why if you build their multiplication tables and try to use them to encrypt and decrypt messages.

Example: Is 2 a good key for a multiplicative cipher?

A. Complete the multiplicative cipher table for key 2.

Times 2 Cipher Table

a	b	c	d	e	f	g	h	i	j	k	l	m	n	o	p	q	r	s	t	u	v	w	x	y	z
0	1	2	3	4	5	6	7	8	9	10	11	12	13	14	15	16	17	18	19	20	21	22	23	24	25
0	2	4																							

B. Use the table to encrypt and decrypt.

Encrypt: Key 2

s	u	e	s		f	u	r	s

Decrypt: Key 2

10	14	8	10

There is a problem with multiplicative key 2. Both **sues** and **furs** encrypt to 10 14 8 10. So you can't be sure how to decrypt.

The number 2 is a **bad key** because it encrypts more than one letter to the same ciphernumber. For example, both **f** and **s** are encrypted to 10. That gives more than one choice of plaintext letter when decrypting. You can't be sure which was the original plaintext.

The number 3 is a **good key** because it encrypts every letter differently, as shown in the times 3 cipher table you constructed on page 41.

1. With your group or class, build multiplicative cipher tables for different keys to investigate which numbers from 1 to 25 are good keys and which are bad. You can use the blank tables on page 82. (You don't need to fill the bottom row.)

2. Use your class's findings to complete this table:

Good Keys	Bad Keys
3,	2,

3. Describe the numbers that make good multiplicative keys.

____

____

Multiplicative Ciphers: Decrypting

Using Inverses

a	b	c	d	e	f	g	h	i	j	k	l	m	n	o	p	q	r	s	t	u	v	w	x	y	z
0	1	2	3	4	5	6	7	8	9	10	11	12	13	14	15	16	17	18	19	20	21	22	23	24	25

To decrypt a multiplicative cipher, you need to undo the multiplication. One way to undo multiplication in regular arithmetic is to divide. But division won't always work in modular arithmetic because you might get fractions—modular arithmetic only uses whole numbers.

Another way to undo multiplication is to multiply by an inverse. For example, the multiplicative inverse of 3 in regular arithmetic is ⅓. If you multiply by 3 and then by ⅓, you get back what you started with, as shown here where we start and end with 10:

$$10 \times \underbrace{3 \times \tfrac{1}{3}}_{=1} = 10$$

That is because $3 \times \frac{1}{3} = 1$, and $10 \times 1 = 10$.

Although you cannot use fractions for inverses in modular arithmetic, some whole numbers act as inverses and can be used to decrypt. An **important property of inverses** is that a number times its inverse is 1. This makes them able to undo multiplication. In modular arithmetic, a number times its inverse is equivalent to 1 (mod 26).

To find the multiplicative inverse of a number in mod 26 arithmetic, look for another number you could multiply it by to get an answer that is equivalent to 1 (mod 26). This is the multiplicative inverse (mod 26) of the original number.

Example: The multiplicative inverse of 3 (mod 26) is 9, since $3 \times 9 = 27 \equiv 1 \pmod{26}$. If you multiply by 3, then by 9, and reduce mod 26, you get back what you started with, as shown here where we start and end with 10:

$$10 \times \underbrace{3 \times 9}_{\equiv 1 \pmod{26}} \equiv 10 \pmod{26}$$

That is because $3 \times 9 \equiv 1 \pmod{26}$, and $10 \times 1 \equiv 10 \pmod{26}$.

This diagram shows the calculations for multiplying by 3, then by 9, and then reducing mod 26, ending with what you started with:

$$10 \xrightarrow{\times 3} 30 \equiv 4 \xrightarrow{\times 9} 36 \equiv 10 \pmod{26}$$

If you multiply by a key to encrypt, you can multiply by the inverse of the key to decrypt, since that will undo the multiplication. The **decryption key** for a multiplicative cipher is the inverse (mod 26) of the key used to encrypt. For example, when the key is 3, the decryption key is 9, as shown in the problems below.

1. Encrypt the following with key 3:

plaintext:	s	p	i	d	e	r
plaintext number:	18	15	8			
times key:	54	45	24			
CIPHERNUMBER:	2	19	24			

2. Decrypt your answer to Problem 1, multiplying by the inverse of the 3, which is 9. Check that you get back the plaintext of Problem 1.

plaintext:	s					
plaintext number:	18	15				
times inverse of key:	18	171				
CIPHERNUMBER:	2	19	24			

Finding Multiplicative Inverses

Inverses are useful in cryptography. If you multiply by a number to encrypt, you can multiply by its multiplicative inverse to decrypt.

The **multiplicative inverse (mod 26)** of a number m is the number n such that $m \times n \equiv 1 \pmod{26}$. Below are a few methods to find inverses.

Method 1. Look for 1 in the bottom row of a cipher table. For example, to find the inverse of 15, make the Times 15 Cipher Table. The table shows that $15 \times 7 \equiv 1 \pmod{26}$. Therefore 7 is the inverse of 15 (mod 26).

Times 15 Cipher Table

a	b	c	d	e	f	g	h	i	j	k	l	m	n	o	p	q	r	s	t	u	v	w	x	y	z
0	1	2	3	4	5	6	7	8	9	10	11	12	13	14	15	16	17	18	19	20	21	22	23	24	25
0	15	4	19	8	23	12	1	16	5	20	9	24	13	2	17	6	21	10	25	14	3	18	7	22	11

Method 2. Make a list of numbers that are equivalent to 1 (mod 26): 27, 53, 79, 105, 131, 157, . . . Then divide each by the key until you get a whole number. For example, the equations at the right show the calculations to find the inverse of 15. We find that $105 \div 15 = 7$. Therefore $15 \times 7 = 105 \equiv 1 \pmod{26}$. This way, we see that 7 is the inverse of 15 without having to write out the whole cipher table.

$27 \div 15 = 1.8$
$53 \div 15 = 3.53\ldots$
$79 \div 15 = 5.26\ldots$
$105 \div 15 = 7$

Method 3. Use inverses you already know. Since $7 \times 15 = 15 \times 7$, once you know that 7 is the inverse of 15, you also know that 15 is the inverse of 7. These two inverses are recorded in the table below.

1. Find the inverse of 5 from the table you made on page 46. Enter your answer in the table of Mod 26 Inverses.

2. Find the inverse of 21 and enter it in the table.

3. Complete the table of Mod 26 Inverses using any of the methods of your choice. It includes all the "good keys" that you listed on page 47.

4. The message below was encrypted with a multiplicative cipher using key 15. Decrypt using the inverse of 15.

$10 \times 7 = 70 \equiv 18 \pmod{26}$

plaintext:	s						
plaintext number:	18						
times inverse of key:	70						
CIPHERNUMBER:	10	14	4	4	8	10	10

Mod 26 Inverses

m	*Inverse of m (Mod 26)*
1	
3	9
5	
7	15
9	
11	
15	7
17	
19	
21	
23	
25	

Multiplicative Ciphers: More Decrypting

a	b	c	d	e	f	g	h	i	j	k	l	m	n	o	p	q	r	s	t	u	v	w	x	y	z
0	1	2	3	4	5	6	7	8	9	10	11	12	13	14	15	16	17	18	19	20	21	22	23	24	25

The answer to each riddle has been encrypted with a multiplicative cipher using the given key. Look up the inverses of the keys in your table of inverses on page 49 and use them to decrypt.

1. **Riddle:** What do sea monsters eat?

   Answer: Encryption key 11. Decryption key _____ .

plaintext:	f	i	s	h										
plaintext number:	5	8	18	7										
times inverse of key:	57	190	304	475										
CIPHERNUMBERS:	3	10	16	25		0	13	7		16	25	10	9	16
CIPHERTEXT: (optional)	D	K	Q	Z		A	N	H		Q	Z	K	J	Q

2. **Riddle:** Why did the jellybean go to school?

   Answer: Encryption key 9. Decryption key _____.

t	o																	
19	14																	
45	66																	
15	22		9	10	18	22	4	10		00		06	04	0	23	15	20	10

3. **Riddle:** Why is 2 + 2 = 5 like your left foot?

   Answer: Encryption key 25. Decryption key _____ .

S	H	’	I		N	M	H		J	S	U	T	H

Multiplicative Ciphers: Cracking

a	b	c	d	e	f	g	h	i	j	k	l	m	n	o	p	q	r	s	t	u	v	w	x	y	z
0	1	2	3	4	5	6	7	8	9	10	11	12	13	14	15	16	17	18	19	20	21	22	23	24	25

If you know how to decrypt some of the letters in a multiplicative cipher message, you might be able to figure out the key and decrypt the rest.

In each problem below, the name of a city and the abbreviation of its state have been encrypted with a multiplicative cipher, but only the names of the cities have been decrypted. Crack the ciphers and figure out the states. Tell what keys were used. In some cases, it might be easier to find the decryption key first.

1. C a n t o n ,
   S A N P W N , M I

   Encryption Key ______

   Decryption Key ______

2. B i l l i n g s ,
   V M X X M N W O , I C

   Encryption Key ______

   Decryption Key ______

3. S p r i n g f i e l d ,
   G F X U N C T U K V B , E W

   Encryption Key ______

   Decryption Key ______

4. S a l e m ,
   K A J I Y , S D

   Encryption Key ______

   Decryption Key ______

Multiplicative Ciphers: Cracking

Using Algebra

a	b	c	d	e	f	g	h	i	j	k	l	m	n	o	p	q	r	s	t	u	v	w	x	y	z
0	1	2	3	4	5	6	7	8	9	10	11	12	13	14	15	16	17	18	19	20	21	22	23	24	25

On this page we take a closer look at Problem 4 from the previous page. The problem doesn't have obvious multiplication patterns, so it is hard to see the key. But algebra can help us find it. The problem is to find which state's abbreviation is encrypted here:

```
s a l e m , ? ?
K A J I Y , S D
```

Solution 1: We can find the key m by solving an equivalence. We know that **l** is encrypted as **J**.

Changing **l** to 11 and **J** to 9, we know that: $m \times 11 \equiv 9 \pmod{26}$.

To solve for m, multiply both sides by the inverse of 11, which is 19:

$$m \times \underbrace{11 \times 19}_{1 \pmod{26}} \equiv 9 \times 19 \pmod{26}$$

$$m \equiv 171 \pmod{26}$$

$$m \equiv 15 \pmod{26}$$

Thus, the encryption key is $m = 15$. So the decryption key is 7.

Solution 2: If we use the encryption of **e** instead of **l**, we would get a different equivalence. Changing **e** to 4 and **I** to 8 gives the equivalence:

$$m \times 4 \equiv 8 \pmod{26}$$

The number 4 does not have an inverse (mod 26) so we can't solve this the way we did in Solution 1. But we can still reason out a solution. List numbers that are equivalent to 8 mod 26: 8, 34, 60, 86, . . . Look for a whole number m such that m times 4 is one of the listed numbers. Although 2 is one solution, 2 is not a good key for a multiplicative cipher so it cannot be the m we are looking for. Since $60 \div 4 = 15$, $m = 15$ is a solution and is the key we are looking for.

---

1. Use the inverse of the key found above to reveal what state Salem is in. ____________________

2. Crack the following messages. In each case, some plaintext letters are given.

A. Encryption key ___ Decryption key ___

```
        d u c k
T A Q O R S U W
```

B. Encryption key ___ Decryption key ___

```
        g o i n g
Q U U V Q U E N Q
```

Multiplicative Ciphers: More Cracking 1

a	b	c	d	e	f	g	h	i	j	k	l	m	n	o	p	q	r	s	t	u	v	w	x	y	z
0	1	2	3	4	5	6	7	8	9	10	11	12	13	14	15	16	17	18	19	20	21	22	23	24	25

Each of the following messages is a common two-word expression. Each has been encrypted with a different multiplicative cipher. Crack each message. Find the encryption and decryption keys.

1. f l i p
   V P S L   I S X W

   Encryption Key ______

   Decryption Key ______

2. h a n d s
   Z A N H Q   H Y I N

   Encryption Key ______

   Decryption Key ______

3. s t e p
   E X Y Z   T A M I

   Encryption Key ______

   Decryption Key ______

4. c a s e
   E A K I   E J C K I T

   Encryption Key ______

   Decryption Key ______

Multiplicative Ciphers: More Cracking 2

a	b	c	d	e	f	g	h	i	j	k	l	m	n	o	p	q	r	s	t	u	v	w	x	y	z
0	1	2	3	4	5	6	7	8	9	10	11	12	13	14	15	16	17	18	19	20	21	22	23	24	25

You can get started cracking these messages using the same tips you used for cracking other substitution ciphers. After you guess a few letters, find the key and decrypt.

1. Tom and Tim are brothers. One wrote this letter to the other. He encrypted it with a multiplicative cipher. Crack the message and tell what key was used.

Encryption Key_____

25 16 00 03   11 04 22 ,

11 02 03 13   18 04 02 03   03 00 25 06 04   25 06 00 05   11 04

20 11 00 11 06 04 13   10 14 11 09.   18 04 02   10 06 05 05   15 16 00 03

20 04 22 16 11 15 06 13 24   19 16 03 18   06 13 11 16 03 16 20 11 06 13 24.

20 16 16   18 04 02   05 00 11 16 03 ,

Who sent the message?__________

11 06 22

What are the call letters for the radio station?__________

2. This message was encrypted with a multiplicative cipher. Use cracking strategies to guess a few letters. Then find the key and decrypt.

Encryption Key_____

02 13 02 15 16 12   00 13 21   01 02 15 22 04 22 03 02 13 14 02

14 20 13 08 10 02 15   00 25 25   03 23 04 13 16 22 .

07 02 13 11 00 06 04 13   09 15 00 13 18 25 04 13

Chapter 5

Vigenère Ciphers

Exploring Patterns 5

The message below was encrypted with a Vigenère cipher, which is different from the substitution ciphers you have learned so far. The methods for those substitution ciphers won't help here. What are some of the signs you see in this message that suggest it was not encrypted with a simple substitution cipher?

A M G X T Z   S V T Y H I C K V I H   K N R

W M Y T   N W H   G G I P O   P   A V Q E T R

W J J F X X B H X X W A   G X X U I G.   J H X

I P R   Z X O R R T Z R   G X X U I G   U N W Z A

S V T Y H I C K V I H,   U N O X V T   M I

P N V S   B B   G G I P O.   L M   H W T L   N

W W W E X   Z M L A D Z Q   X D   M A G G G C X.

J A R   E   A W A K T Z   B R T   B B   Q P S R   E

B M F W P O R   L P Z Q I G   B B   G G I P O.

Frequency in message	
Letter	%
G	8.3
X	8.3
I	6.7
W	6.1
R	5.6
T	5.6
A	5.0
B	5.0
P	5.0
H	4.4
Z	4.4
M	3.9
V	3.9
N	3.3
O	3.3
E	2.2
J	2.2
K	2.2
L	2.2
Q	2.2
S	2.2
U	2.2
C	1.7
Y	1.7
D	1.1
F	1.1

List ways this differs from a simple substitution message:

Vigenère Ciphers: Encrypting and Decrypting

Using Cipher Wheels

A **Vigenère cipher** is made by combining different Caesar ciphers according to a **keyword.** It was used in the American Civil War and was once believed to be unbreakable. Although the Vigenère cipher uses a keyword, it is not the same as the cipher called the "keyword cipher."

To use a Vigenère cipher, write the keyword repeatedly above the message. For each letter of the keyword, set the cipher wheel to show the Caesar cipher that matches **a** to that letter. Then use that setting of the wheel to encrypt/decrypt every letter that has that keyword letter above it.

Example: Encrypt **undercover agent** with keyword **SPY.**

✓ **STEP 1:** Write the keyword above the letters of your message.

✓ **STEP 2:** Use the **a** - **S** wheel to encrypt every letter with **S** above it. (See table.)

STEP 3: Use the **a** - **P** wheel to encrypt every letter with **P** above it.

STEP 4: Use the **a** - **Y** wheel to encrypt every letter with **Y** above it.

Don't write anything above blank spaces or punctuation.

keyword:	S	P	Y	S	P	Y	S	P	Y	S		P	Y	S	P	Y
plaintext:	u	n	d	e	r	c	o	v	e	r		a	g	e	n	t
CIPHERTEXT:	M			W			G			J				W		

*The **a**-**S** wheel matches **a** with **S**, the first letter of the keyword.*

The ***a*** - ***S*** wheel

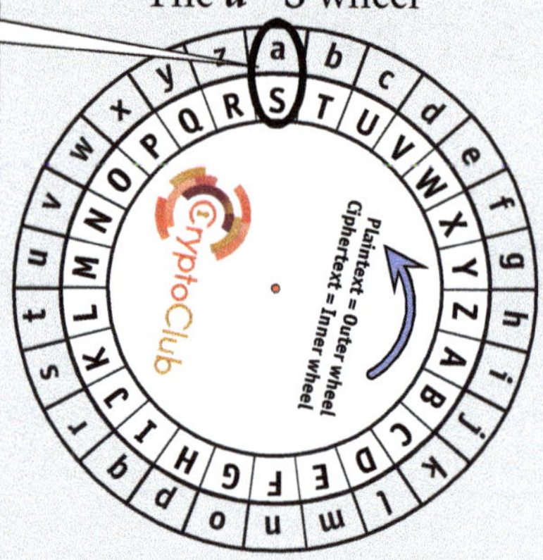

The ***a*** - ***P*** wheel

The ***a*** - ***Y*** wheel

1. Finish encrypting the message in the example.
2. Decrypt the following using keyword **SPY:**

keyword:	S															
plaintext:	k															
CIPHERTEXT:	C	T	C	H		I	F	A	H		Q	W	R	P	W	I

Vigenère Ciphers: Encrypting and Decrypting

Using Vigenère Squares

You can use a Vigenère square as a tool to encrypt and decrypt with a Vigenère cipher instead of using a cipher wheel. The basic steps are.

To encrypt/decrypt, write the keyword repeatedly above the message, as you did with cipher wheels. Then, for each letter of the keyword, choose the row in the table that begins with that letter. Use that row to encrypt/decrypt every letter that has that keyword letter above it.

To **encrypt using a chosen row**: Begin in the top row with the plaintext letter you want to encrypt. Follow its column down to the letter where it meets the chosen row.

To **decrypt using a chosen row**: Begin in the chosen row with the ciphertext letter you want to decrypt. Follow its column up to the plaintext letter it meets in the top row.

Example: The figure shows how to encrypt the first letter in Problem 1.

To encrypt plaintext ***t*** *using Row D, begin in the top row.*

	a	b	c	d	e	f	g	h	i	j	k	l	m	n	o	p	q	r	s	t	u	v	w	x	y	z
0	A	B	C	D	E	F	G	H	I	J	K	L	M	N	O	P	Q	R	S	T	U	V	W	X	Y	Z
1	B	C	D	E	F	G	H	I	J	K	L	M	N	O	P	Q	R	S	T	U	V	W	X	Y	Z	A
2	C	D	E	F	G	H	I	J	K	L	M	N	O	P	Q	R	S	T	U	V	W	X	Y	Z	A	B
3	D	E	F	G	H	I	J	K	L	M	N	O	P	Q	R	S	T	U	V	**W**	X	Y	Z	A	B	C
4	E	F	G	H	I	J	K	L	M	N	O	P	Q	R	S	T	U	V	W	X	Y	Z	A	B	C	D
5	F	G	H	I	J	K	L	M	N	O	P	Q	R	S	T	U	V	W	X	Y	Z	A	B	C	D	E
6	G	H	I	J	K	L	M	N	O	P	Q	R	S	T	U	V	W	X	Y	Z	A	B	C	D	E	F
7	H	I	J	K	L	M	N	O	P	Q	R	S	T	U	V	W	X	Y	Z	A	B	C	D	E	F	G
8	I	J	K	L	M	N	O	P	Q	R	S	T	U	V	W	X	Y	Z	A	B	C	D	E	F	G	H
9	J	K	L	M	N	O	P	Q	R	S	T	U	V	W	X	Y	Z	A	B	C	D	E	F	G	H	I
10	K	L	M	N	O	P	Q	R	S	T	U	V	W	X	Y	Z	A	B	C	D	E	F	G	H	I	J
11	L	M	N	O	P	Q	R	S	T	U	V	W	X	Y	Z	A	B	C	D	E	F	G	H	I	J	K
12	M	N	O	P	Q	R	S	T	U	V	W	X	Y	Z	A	B	C	D	E	F	G	H	I	J	K	L
13	N	O	P	Q	R	S	T	U	V	W	X	Y	Z	A	B	C	D	E	F	G	H	I	J	K	L	M
14	O	P	Q	R	S	T	U	V	W	X	Y	Z	A	B	C	D	E	F	G	H	I	J	K	L	M	N
15	P	Q	R	S	T	U	V	W	X	Y	Z	A	B	C	D	E	F	G	H	I	J	K	L	M	N	O
16	Q	R	S	T	U	V	W	X	Y	Z	A	B	C	D	E	F	G	H	I	J	K	L	M	N	O	P
17	R	S	T	U	V	W	X	Y	Z	A	B	C	D	E	F	G	H	I	J	K	L	M	N	O	P	Q
18	S	T	U	V	W	X	Y	Z	A	B	C	D	E	F	G	H	I	J	K	L	M	N	O	P	Q	R
19	T	U	V	W	X	Y	Z	A	B	C	D	E	F	G	H	I	J	K	L	M	N	O	P	Q	R	S
20	U	V	W	X	Y	Z	A	B	C	D	E	F	G	H	I	J	K	L	M	N	O	P	Q	R	S	T
21	V	W	X	Y	Z	A	B	C	D	E	F	G	H	I	J	K	L	M	N	O	P	Q	R	S	T	U
22	W	X	Y	Z	A	B	C	D	E	F	G	H	I	J	K	L	M	N	O	P	Q	R	S	T	U	V
23	X	Y	Z	A	B	C	D	E	F	G	H	I	J	K	L	M	N	O	P	Q	R	S	T	U	V	W
24	Y	Z	A	B	C	D	E	F	G	H	I	J	K	L	M	N	O	P	Q	R	S	T	U	V	W	X
25	Z	A	B	C	D	E	F	G	H	I	J	K	L	M	N	O	P	Q	R	S	T	U	V	W	X	Y

End with ciphertext ***W****, the letter where Row D and the column under* ***t*** *meet.*

1. Encrypt the following with keyword DOG. Use the Vigenère square.

keyword:	D	O	G	D		O	G	D	O		G	D	O	G							
plaintext:	t	i	m	e		w	i	l	l		t	e	l	l							
CIPHERTEXT:	W																				

2. Decrypt the following with keyword DOG. Use the Vigenère square.

keyword:	D																				
plaintext:	i																				
CIPHERTEXT:	L	A	V	R	F	Z	D	B	Z		L	B	L	R	F	S	D	H	O	R	B

Vigenère Ciphers: More Encrypting

For each problem, think of an item from the category and write it in the plaintext boxes. Choose a keyword and encrypt with that keyword.

Example: Something good to eat

Keyword KEY

keyword:	K	E	Y	K																		
plaintext:	m	a	s	h	e	d		p	o	t	a	t	o	e	s							
ciphertext:	W	E	Q	R																		

1. Something good to eat

Keyword ________________

keyword:																						
plaintext:																						
CIPHERTEXT:																						

2. Something you would like to change

Keyword ________________

keyword:																						
plaintext:																						
CIPHERTEXT:																						

3. Something with stripes

Keyword ________________

keyword:																						
plaintext:																						
CIPHERTEXT:																						

Vigenère Ciphers: More Decrypting

Decrypt these messages that were encrypted with a Vigenère Cipher.

Message 1 Keyword **ROAD**

Z T   Y R L   R O Q ' K   Y N R N   K H H I S

Y R L   O R H   X C I Q X ,   O N B   I C A G

N W L O   X S T   B F I   T K V F E .

O V K I V   T O R U F Z L

Message 2 Keyword **SKY**

K Y K W G F W B C ,   K Y K W D F A X E

A X A J O B A L J W   S Q   O K G L S L Y

D M   T O   I F Y U F .   M Y J V   Q S Q Y F

Vigenère Ciphers: Cracking

Part 1 Finding the Keylength

The Vigenère Cipher was once believed to be unbreakable. But now ways are known to crack it. You can often find patterns in a Vigenère message that can help you guess the keylength.

Example: Below is the ciphertext from a Vigenère message. Note that it has a repeated string of letters, **WVK**. Examining why repeated strings occur can help to develop a method for guessing keylengths.

WVK VIT, WVK PCUQ, OTG HNH GZDFY

The most likely reason for repeated strings of letters in the ciphertext is that they came from encrypting repeated strings of plaintext letters. But the same plaintext letters aren't always encrypted as the same letters by a Vigenère cipher. If they are, then they must have the same letters of the keyword above them.

The keyword lines up the same way above two strings of letters if the number of letters between them—from the start of one to the start of the other—is a multiple of the keylength.

Below you can see the plaintext and keyword **DOG** that were used to get the ciphertext. Note that the number of letters from the start of the first **the** to the start of the second **the** is 6, which is a multiple of the keylength, 3. The third **the** does not encrypt to **WVK** because its distance from other occurrences of **the** is not a multiple of the keylength.

```
D O G   D O G   D O G   D O G D,   O G D   O G D   O G D O G
t h e   s u n,  t h e   m o o n,   a n d   t h e   s t a r s
W V K   V I T,  W V K   P C U Q,   O T G   H N H   G Z D F Y
```

A good way to guess the keylength is to find pairs of repeated strings in the ciphertext and then find the distances between them. Since the distances are probably multiples of the keylength, the keylength is probably a common factor of the distances.

1. Circle several pairs of repeated strings in the message below.

WSMJOQNBD QSQYSOX QXS VBQD VTI

QT TFSR X UCPXWYQS HJMIJBDYV CTF

VTIO RSPXODJ. BLB MLZ QXS TFSWPM.

2. Find and factor the distances between the repeated strings. Complete the table.

String	Distance	Factorization

3. What is a likely keylength? ________

Vigenère Ciphers: Cracking

Part 2 Cracking When You Know the Keylength

If you know the length of the key used to encrypt a Vigenère message, you can figure out which letters were encrypted with the same shift of the Caesar cipher wheel. Then you can divide up the message into groups that were encrypted with the same shift and crack each group separately.

Example. The message from the previous page is shown below. You probably figured out that the keylength is likely to be 3. If that is correct, then every third letter was encrypted with the same shift of the Caesar cipher wheel. We wrote **1 2 3** repeatedly under the message to show the letters that were encrypted with the same shift.

r			e			i				l			t			s				n				l	
W	S	M	J	O	Q	N	B	D		Q	S	Q	Y	S	O	X		Q	X	S		V	B	Q	D
1	2	3	1	2	3	1	2	3		1	2	3	1	2	3	1		2	3	1		2	3	1	2

V	T	I		Q	T		T	F	S	R		X		U	C	P	X	W	Y	Q	S				
3	1	2		3	1		2	3	1	2		3		1	2	3	1	2	3	1	2				

H	J	M	I	J	B	D	Y	V		C	T	F		V	T	I	O		R	S	P	X	O	D	J.
3	1	2	3	1	2	3	1	2		3	1	2		3	1	2	3		1	2	3	1	2	3	1

B	L	B		M	L	Z		Q	X	S		T	F	S	W	P	M.								
2	3	1		2	3	1		2	3	1		2	3	1	2	3	1								

Decrypt the letters with 1 underneath: If you tally up the frequency of the letters that have 1 underneath as shown below, you will find that the most common letters in this group are **J**, **S**, and **T**. Try matching **J** with **e**, and use this wheel to decrypt the rest of the letters with 1 underneath. The first line of letters of this group are done for you above.

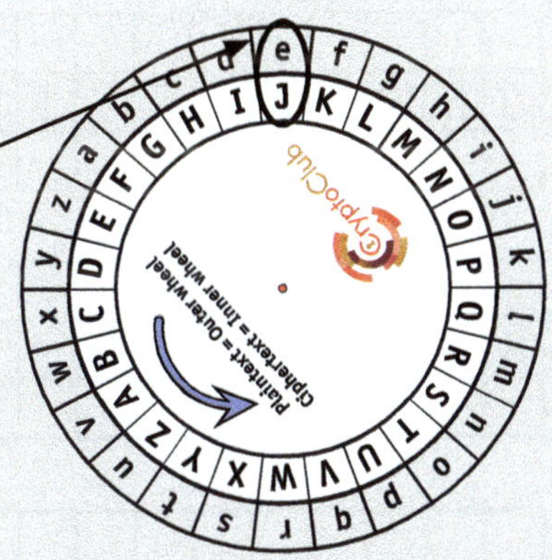

W I	**Y** I	**U** I	**M** I
Try *e* →**J** IIII	**X** III	**R** I	
N I	**S** IIII	**B** I	
Q III	**T** IIII	**Z** I	

1. Finish decrypting the letters with 1 underneath.
2. Decrypt the letters with 2 underneath. First find the most common letters with 2 underneath to help you decide how to set the cipher wheel.
3. Decrypt the letters with 3 underneath. You might be able to guess a letter without finding frequencies, since the message is partly decrypted.

Vigenère Ciphers: More Cracking

1. Below is the message that you first saw on page 57. Circle several pairs of strings of letters that repeat in the message. Find and factor the distances between them.

String	Distance	Factorization

What is a likely keylength? ______

2. Write numbers under the message to indicate the letters that were encrypted with the same Caesar cipher. Crack the message.

A M G X T Z S V T Y H I C K V I H K N R W M Y T N W H

G G I P O P A V Q E T R W J J F X X B H X X W A

G X X U I G . J H X I P R Z X O R R T Z R G X X U I G

U N W Z A S V T Y H I C K V I H , U N O X V T M I P N V S

B B G G I P O . L M H W T L N W W W E X Z M L A D Z Q

X D M A G G G C X . J A R E A W A K T Z B R T B B

Q P S R E B M F W P O R L P Z Q I G B B G G I P O .

Chapter 6

Affine Ciphers

Exploring Patterns 6

1. The 12 words below were encrypted with the same cipher. Figure out the words and use the cipher table to show how the letters were encrypted. Find a pattern to complete the table.

j	u	l	y
2	9	8	21

1	9	19	9	3	6

2	9	14	13

3	13	20	6	13	11	4	13	0

2	1	14	9	1	0	21

16	13	4	0	9	1	0	21

14	17	12	13	11	4	13	0

11	1	0	7	22

11	1	21

1	20	0	25	8

10	13	7	13	11	4	13	0

17	7	6	17	4	13	0

Cipher Table

a	b	c	d	e	f	g	h	i	j	k	l	m	n	o	p	q	r	s	t	u	v	w	x	y	z
0	1	2	3	4	5	6	7	8	9	10	11	12	13	14	15	16	17	18	19	20	21	22	23	24	25
									2		*8*									*9*				*21*	

2. Use the cipher table to decrypt the following message:

07 01 14   21 17 09   16 25 19 09 00 13   17 09 06   22 17 15   15 13

09 03 13 10   04 17 06 22   11 09 08 06 25 20 08 25 07 01 06 25 17 14

01 14 10   01 10 10 25 06 25 17 14   06 17   13 14 07 00 21 20 06 ?

Affine Ciphers: Encrypting

a	b	c	d	e	f	g	h	i	j	k	l	m	n	o	p	q	r	s	t	u	v	w	x	y	z
0	1	2	3	4	5	6	7	8	9	10	11	12	13	14	15	16	17	18	19	20	21	22	23	24	25

The cipher used on the previous page was an affine cipher with multiplicative key 3 and additive key 1.

An affine cipher is a cipher that combines multiplication and addition. You will need a good multiplicative key m and an additive key b. To encrypt with an **affine cipher** using key (m, b), first change your message to numbers. Next multiply each number by m, then add b. Finally, reduce mod 26. Convert to letters if you like.

See page 49 for good multiplicative keys.

Example: Encrypt the following using the affine cipher with key (3, 5).

Multiply by $m = 3$, then add $b = 5$.

The steps can be shown in one equation:

$(3 \times 20 + 5) \bmod 26 = 13$

plaintext:	u	n	d	e	r
plaintext number:	20				
times m:	60				
plus b:	65				
CIPHERNUMBER (reduce mod 26):	13				
CIPHERTEXT:	N				

1. Finish encrypting the following using the affine cipher with key (3, 5), so $m = 3$ and $b = 5$.

plaintext:	a	r	o	u	n	d
plaintext number:	0	17				
times m:	0	51				
plus b:	5	56				
CIPHERNUMBER:	5	4				
CIPHERTEXT:	F	E				

2. Encrypt the following using the affine cipher with key (7, 8).

plaintext:	t	h	r	o	u	g	h
plaintext number:							
times m:							
plus b:							
CIPHERNUMBER:							
CIPHERTEXT:							

3. Write an equation that shows how you encrypted the letter **r** in Problem 2.

____

Affine Ciphers: More Encrypting

a	b	c	d	e	f	g	h	i	j	k	l	m	n	o	p	q	r	s	t	u	v	w	x	y	z
0	1	2	3	4	5	6	7	8	9	10	11	12	13	14	15	16	17	18	19	20	21	22	23	24	25

For each problem, think of an item from the category and write it in the plaintext boxes. Choose an affine key and encrypt. Convert to letters if you like. Later you can use your answers in a class game.

Example: Something you shouldn't doodle on

Key (5, 8)

plaintext:	s	c	h	o	o	l		d	e	s	k
plaintext number:	18	2								18	10
CIPHERNUMBER:	20 ~~98~~	18								20 ~~98~~	6 ~~58~~
CIPHERTEXT: (optional)	U									U	G

1. Something you shouldn't doodle on

Key (______, ______)

plaintext:																		
plaintext number:																		
CIPHERNUMBER:																		

2. Something you shouldn't do with glue

Key (______, ______)

plaintext:																		
plaintext number:																		
CIPHERNUMBER:																		

Affine Ciphers: Decrypting

a	b	c	d	e	f	g	h	i	j	k	l	m	n	o	p	q	r	s	t	u	v	w	x	y	z
0	1	2	3	4	5	6	7	8	9	10	11	12	13	14	15	16	17	18	19	20	21	22	23	24	25

If a message was encrypted using the affine cipher with the key (m, b), you need to "undo" the encryption steps to decrypt. Start with the last step and go backward. To encrypt, someone multiplied by m and added b. So, to go backward, you should subtract b and then multiply by the mod 26 inverse of m, which we write as m^{-1}.

Example: Encrypt the letter **s** with the affine cipher with the key (3, 5). Then decrypt the answer.

To **encrypt**, change the plaintext letter to a number. Then multiply by $m = 3$ and add $b = 5$. The encrypting steps are shown below. The answer is **H**.

plaintext:	s
plaintext number:	18
times m:	54
plus b:	59
CIPHERNUMBER:	7
CIPHERTEXT:	H

To encrypt, start with ***s*** *and work down the table.*

To **decrypt,** change the ciphertext letter to a number. Then subtract $b = 5$, and multiply by the mod 26 inverse of 3, which is 9. The decrypting steps are shown below. Follow the steps to get back **s.**

plaintext:	s
plaintext number:	18
times m^{-1}:	18
minus b:	2
CIPHERNUMBER:	7
CIPHERTEXT:	H

m^{-1} is the inverse of m.

To decrypt, start with ***H*** *and work up the table.*

Decrypt the following words that were encrypted with affine ciphers.

1. Key (3, 6), so $m = 3$ and $b = 6$.

plaintext:	b			
plaintext number:	1			
times inverse of m:	27			
minus b:	3			
CIPHERNUMBER:	9			
CIPHERTEXT:	J	G	M	K

2. Key (15, 8), so $m = 15$ and $b = 8$.

plaintext:				
plaintext number:				
times m^{-1}:				
minus b:				
CIPHERNUMBER:				
CIPHERTEXT:	H	I	M	C

Since $m = 15$, $m^{-1} = 7$.

Affine Ciphers: More Decrypting 1

a	b	c	d	e	f	g	h	i	j	k	l	m	n	o	p	q	r	s	t	u	v	w	x	y	z
0	1	2	3	4	5	6	7	8	9	10	11	12	13	14	15	16	17	18	19	20	21	22	23	24	25

Decrypt the answer to each riddle.

1. **Riddle:** What do you call a fish without an eye?
   Answer: Encrypted with key (21, 10).

plaintext:					
plaintext number:					
times m^{-1}:					
minus b:					
CIPHERNUMBER:					
CIPHERTEXT:	K		L	Y	B

$m =$ ______

$m^{-1} =$ ______

$b =$ ______

2. **Riddle:** What kind of snake is good at math?
   Answer: Encrypted with key (9, 7).

7	20		7	8	8	17	4

$m =$ ______

$m^{-1} =$ ______

$b =$ ______

3. **Riddle:** What has no arms and no head but hands and a face?
   Answer: Encrypted with key (5, 20).

U		E	X	M	E	S

$m =$ ______

$m^{-1} =$ ______

$b =$ ______

Affine Ciphers: Encrypting and Decrypting

Using Formulas

a	b	c	d	e	f	g	h	i	j	k	l	m	n	o	p	q	r	s	t	u	v	w	x	y	z
0	1	2	3	4	5	6	7	8	9	10	11	12	13	14	15	16	17	18	19	20	21	22	23	24	25

You can use mathematical formulas to show the encrypting and decrypting steps of an affine cipher. If (m, b) is the key, then this formula tells how to encrypt a plaintext number x to get a ciphernumber Y:

Affine Encryption Formula

$$Y = (mx + b) \bmod 26$$

Solving the encryption formula for x gives:

Affine Decryption Formula

$$x = (Y - b) \times m^{-1} \bmod 26$$

m^{-1} is the inverse of m.

Example 1: Encrypt plaintext **t** with the affine cipher using key (7, 6). The encrypting formula for this key is

$$Y = (7x + 6) \bmod 26.$$

To encrypt **t**, change **t** to the plaintext number **19**, and apply the encrypting formula:

$$Y = (7 \times 19 + 6) \bmod 26 = 139 \bmod 26 = 9$$

Since 9 corresponds to the letter **J**, **t** is encrypted as **J**.

Example 2: Decrypt ciphertext **J** with the affine cipher using key (7, 6). With $m = 7$, $m^{-1} = 15$, so the decrypting formula for this key is

$$x = (Y - 6) \times 15 \bmod 26$$

Since **J** corresponds to 9, we substitute $Y = 9$ and get $x = 19$, which corresponds to **t**.

1. Encrypt with key (7, 2).
   A. Write the affine encryption formula for this key:________________________________.
   B. Encrypt using your formula:

plaintext:	p	i	z	z	a
plaintext number:					
CIPHERNUMBER:					
CIPHERTEXT:					

2. Decrypt the answer to the riddle below. It was encrypted with key (9, 6).
   A. Write the affine decryption formula for this key: ________________________________.
   B. Decrypt using your formula:

Riddle: What is the best thing to part with?
Answer:

plaintext:						
plaintext number:						
CIPHERNUMBER:						
CIPHERTEXT:	G		Y	C	K	P

Affine Ciphers: More Decrypting 2

a	b	c	d	e	f	g	h	i	j	k	l	m	n	o	p	q	r	s	t	u	v	w	x	y	z
0	1	2	3	4	5	6	7	8	9	10	11	12	13	14	15	16	17	18	19	20	21	22	23	24	25

Decrypt the answer to each riddle. Each has been encrypted with an affine cipher. Write the affine decrypting formula.

1. **Riddle:** What kind of cheese is made backwards?
   Answer:

   Key (19, 11)
   Affine decryption formula:

   ____

   09 16 11 05

2. **Riddle:** What do you call a cat drinking lemonade?
   Answer:

   Key (17, 4)
   Affine decryption formula:

   ____

   04 24 08 06 07 25 06 24 24

3. **Riddle:** What has six eyes but cannot see?
   Answer:

   Key (9, 4)
   Affine decryption formula:

   ____

   19 15 01 14 14 13 25 24 17 05 08 24 22 14

4. **Riddle:** Why did I take a prune to the dance?
   Answer:

   Key (21, 20)
   Affine decryption formula:

   ____

   06 10 02 24 17 05 07 ' 03 21 06 07 05

   20 05 20 03 00

Affine Ciphers: Cracking

a	b	c	d	e	f	g	h	i	j	k	l	m	n	o	p	q	r	s	t	u	v	w	x	y	z
0	1	2	3	4	5	6	7	8	9	10	11	12	13	14	15	16	17	18	19	20	21	22	23	24	25

In each problem, an affine cipher was used to encrypt the name of a book and its author. The author's name has already been decrypted. Crack the code to find the name of the book.

Use the table below each problem to show how the known letters were encrypted. Find a pattern in the table that will help you find the affine key.

1. Key (_____,_____)

Encryption formula ____________________

Decryption formula ____________________

by B a b b i t

23 20 22 24 16 17 16 03 21 02 00 23 04 15 10 *by* 25 02 25 25 04 23

a	b	c	d	e	f	g	h	i	j	k	l	m	n	o	p	q	r	s	t	u	v	w	x	y	z
0	1	2	3	4	5	6	7	8	9	10	11	12	13	14	15	16	17	18	19	20	21	22	23	24	25
02	25							04											23						

2. Key (_____,_____)

Encryption formula ____________________

Decryption formula ____________________

by s a c h a r

17 00 11 02 20 *by* 20 08 18 17 08 15

a	b	c	d	e	f	g	h	i	j	k	l	m	n	o	p	q	r	s	t	u	v	w	x	y	z
0	1	2	3	4	5	6	7	8	9	10	11	12	13	14	15	16	17	18	19	20	21	22	23	24	25

3. Key (_____,_____)

Encryption formula ____________________

Decryption formula ____________________

by l ' e n g l e

06 20 05 04 19 10 13 18 04 19 11 04 16 18 *by* 13 ' 18 19 24 13 18

a	b	c	d	e	f	g	h	i	j	k	l	m	n	o	p	q	r	s	t	u	v	w	x	y	z
0	1	2	3	4	5	6	7	8	9	10	11	12	13	14	15	16	17	18	19	20	21	22	23	24	25

Affine Ciphers: Cracking Using Algebra

a	b	c	d	e	f	g	h	i	j	k	l	m	n	o	p	q	r	s	t	u	v	w	x	y	z
0	1	2	3	4	5	6	7	8	9	10	11	12	13	14	15	16	17	18	19	20	21	22	23	24	25

If we don't know the key used to encrypt a message with an affine cipher, we can use algebra to find it.

Example: Elsa decrypted most of this message, using frequency analysis and common sense. But she didn't know which radio station. We can figure it out because we know some of the plaintext.

*l was encrypted to **V**. Changing to numbers, 11 was encrypted to 21.*

*i was encrypted to **E**. Changing to numbers, 8 was encrypted to 4.*

l i s t e n	t o	r a d i o	s t a t i o n	w ? ? ?
V E A X Q P	X M	D C T E M	A X C X E M P	O Y G A

We can write equivalences that show how these letters were encrypted, using the unknown key, m and b. We can then solve for m and b:

Since **11** encrypts to **21** we get the equivalence: $m \times 11 + b \equiv 21 \pmod{26}$

Since **8** encrypts to **4** we get another equivalence: $m \times 8 + b \equiv 4 \pmod{26}$

One way to solve for m and b is to subtract the two equivalences. Subtracting gives: $m \times 3 \equiv 17 \pmod{26}$

To solve for m we multiply both sides by the inverse of 3 (mod 26), which is 9:

$$m \times \underbrace{3 \times 9}_{1 \bmod 26} \equiv \underbrace{17 \times 9}_{23 \bmod 26} \pmod{26}$$

$$m \equiv 23 \pmod{26}$$

To find b, we can now subsitute $m = 23$ into the first equivalence:

$$\underbrace{23 \times 11}_{253 \equiv 19 \pmod{26}} + b \equiv 21 \pmod{26}$$

$$19 + b \equiv 21 \pmod{26}$$

Subtract 19 from both sides: $b \equiv 2 \pmod{26}$

Therefore, $(m, b) = (23, 2)$. Since $23^{-1} = 17$, the decrypting formula is $x = (Y - 2) \times 17 \bmod 26$. The first unknown letter to decrypt is **Y**:

$$\mathbf{Y} \rightarrow 24\ ;\ (24 - 2) \times 17 = 22 \times 17 = 374 \equiv 10 \pmod{26} \rightarrow \mathbf{k}$$

1. What are all of the plaintext letters for the radio station in Elsa's message?____________________
2. Find the missing word in this partially decrypted message.

Key (____,____)

t	h	i	s		i	s		f	o	r						
X	P	U	S		U	S		F	Y	N		J	C	Q	G	S

Affine Ciphers: More Cracking 1

a	b	c	d	e	f	g	h	i	j	k	l	m	n	o	p	q	r	s	t	u	v	w	x	y	z
0	1	2	3	4	5	6	7	8	9	10	11	12	13	14	15	16	17	18	19	20	21	22	23	24	25

Each of the following is the name of a book, followed by the author's last name. Each has been encrypted with a different affine cipher. You can figure out the key for each one because the author's name has already been decrypted. Use algebra to figure out the key and decrypt.

Key (____,____)

r i o r d a n

1. I O J I H I L Y ' P X B W P J *by* W H R W Q L Y

Key (____,____)

g a i m a n

2. C Y X P K N U X V N K O W J J Z *by* P N H R N A

Key (____,____)

l o w r y

3. S O N F X K N A *by* Y Z T A L

Key (____,____)

m e y e r

4. D K M T M Q B D *by* E U G U H

Affine Ciphers: More Cracking 2

a	b	c	d	e	f	g	h	i	j	k	l	m	n	o	p	q	r	s	t	u	v	w	x	y	z
0	1	2	3	4	5	6	7	8	9	10	11	12	13	14	15	16	17	18	19	20	21	22	23	24	25

Crack the following message, which was encrypted with an affine cipher.

As you decrypt, enter the substitutions in the table below the message. Figure out the key. You can use the affine encrypting formula for letters you cannot guess.

Key (____,____)

21 05 03 05 15 19 09 09 13 15 15 04 07 24 05 01

20 13 09 05 19 15 13 21 06 05 24 05 02 00 21 13 18 24

23 06 07 20 13 14 21 13 08 13 24 21 18 03 13 05 18 24

21 24 21 24 18 ' 04 06 05 08 13 04 06 13 06 13 05 00 04

04 07 14 13 04 06 21 03 24 07 23 18 .

—Abraham Lincoln

Cipher Table

a	b	c	d	e	f	g	h	i	j	k	l	m	n	o	p	q	r	s	t	u	v	w	x	y	z
0	1	2	3	4	5	6	7	8	9	10	11	12	13	14	15	16	17	18	19	20	21	22	23	24	25

Appendix

Cryptography Tools and Tables

Cipher Tables

Here are extra tables to use when encrypting and decrypting other messages.

a	b	c	d	e	f	g	h	i	j	k	l	m	n	o	p	q	r	s	t	u	v	w	x	y	z

a	b	c	d	e	f	g	h	i	j	k	l	m	n	o	p	q	r	s	t	u	v	w	x	y	z

a	b	c	d	e	f	g	h	i	j	k	l	m	n	o	p	q	r	s	t	u	v	w	x	y	z

a	b	c	d	e	f	g	h	i	j	k	l	m	n	o	p	q	r	s	t	u	v	w	x	y	z

a	b	c	d	e	f	g	h	i	j	k	l	m	n	o	p	q	r	s	t	u	v	w	x	y	z

a	b	c	d	e	f	g	h	i	j	k	l	m	n	o	p	q	r	s	t	u	v	w	x	y	z

a	b	c	d	e	f	g	h	i	j	k	l	m	n	o	p	q	r	s	t	u	v	w	x	y	z

a	b	c	d	e	f	g	h	i	j	k	l	m	n	o	p	q	r	s	t	u	v	w	x	y	z

a	b	c	d	e	f	g	h	i	j	k	l	m	n	o	p	q	r	s	t	u	v	w	x	y	z

a	b	c	d	e	f	g	h	i	j	k	l	m	n	o	p	q	r	s	t	u	v	w	x	y	z

a	b	c	d	e	f	g	h	i	j	k	l	m	n	o	p	q	r	s	t	u	v	w	x	y	z

Cipher Tables for Numbers

a	b	c	d	e	f	g	h	i	j	k	l	m	n	o	p	q	r	s	t	u	v	w	x	y	z
0	1	2	3	4	5	6	7	8	9	10	11	12	13	14	15	16	17	18	19	20	21	22	23	24	25

a	b	c	d	e	f	g	h	i	j	k	l	m	n	o	p	q	r	s	t	u	v	w	x	y	z
0	1	2	3	4	5	6	7	8	9	10	11	12	13	14	15	16	17	18	19	20	21	22	23	24	25

a	b	c	d	e	f	g	h	i	j	k	l	m	n	o	p	q	r	s	t	u	v	w	x	y	z
0	1	2	3	4	5	6	7	8	9	10	11	12	13	14	15	16	17	18	19	20	21	22	23	24	25

a	b	c	d	e	f	g	h	i	j	k	l	m	n	o	p	q	r	s	t	u	v	w	x	y	z
0	1	2	3	4	5	6	7	8	9	10	11	12	13	14	15	16	17	18	19	20	21	22	23	24	25

a	b	c	d	e	f	g	h	i	j	k	l	m	n	o	p	q	r	s	t	u	v	w	x	y	z
0	1	2	3	4	5	6	7	8	9	10	11	12	13	14	15	16	17	18	19	20	21	22	23	24	25

a	b	c	d	e	f	g	h	i	j	k	l	m	n	o	p	q	r	s	t	u	v	w	x	y	z
0	1	2	3	4	5	6	7	8	9	10	11	12	13	14	15	16	17	18	19	20	21	22	23	24	25

a	b	c	d	e	f	g	h	i	j	k	l	m	n	o	p	q	r	s	t	u	v	w	x	y	z
0	1	2	3	4	5	6	7	8	9	10	11	12	13	14	15	16	17	18	19	20	21	22	23	24	25

Cipher Tables for Numbers

a	b	c	d	e	f	g	h	i	j	k	l	m	n	o	p	q	r	s	t	u	v	w	x	y	z
0	1	2	3	4	5	6	7	8	9	10	11	12	13	14	15	16	17	18	19	20	21	22	23	24	25

a	b	c	d	e	f	g	h	i	j	k	l	m	n	o	p	q	r	s	t	u	v	w	x	y	z
0	1	2	3	4	5	6	7	8	9	10	11	12	13	14	15	16	17	18	19	20	21	22	23	24	25

a	b	c	d	e	f	g	h	i	j	k	l	m	n	o	p	q	r	s	t	u	v	w	x	y	z
0	1	2	3	4	5	6	7	8	9	10	11	12	13	14	15	16	17	18	19	20	21	22	23	24	25

a	b	c	d	e	f	g	h	i	j	k	l	m	n	o	p	q	r	s	t	u	v	w	x	y	z
0	1	2	3	4	5	6	7	8	9	10	11	12	13	14	15	16	17	18	19	20	21	22	23	24	25

a	b	c	d	e	f	g	h	i	j	k	l	m	n	o	p	q	r	s	t	u	v	w	x	y	z
0	1	2	3	4	5	6	7	8	9	10	11	12	13	14	15	16	17	18	19	20	21	22	23	24	25

a	b	c	d	e	f	g	h	i	j	k	l	m	n	o	p	q	r	s	t	u	v	w	x	y	z
0	1	2	3	4	5	6	7	8	9	10	11	12	13	14	15	16	17	18	19	20	21	22	23	24	25

a	b	c	d	e	f	g	h	i	j	k	l	m	n	o	p	q	r	s	t	u	v	w	x	y	z
0	1	2	3	4	5	6	7	8	9	10	11	12	13	14	15	16	17	18	19	20	21	22	23	24	25

Mod 26 Spiral

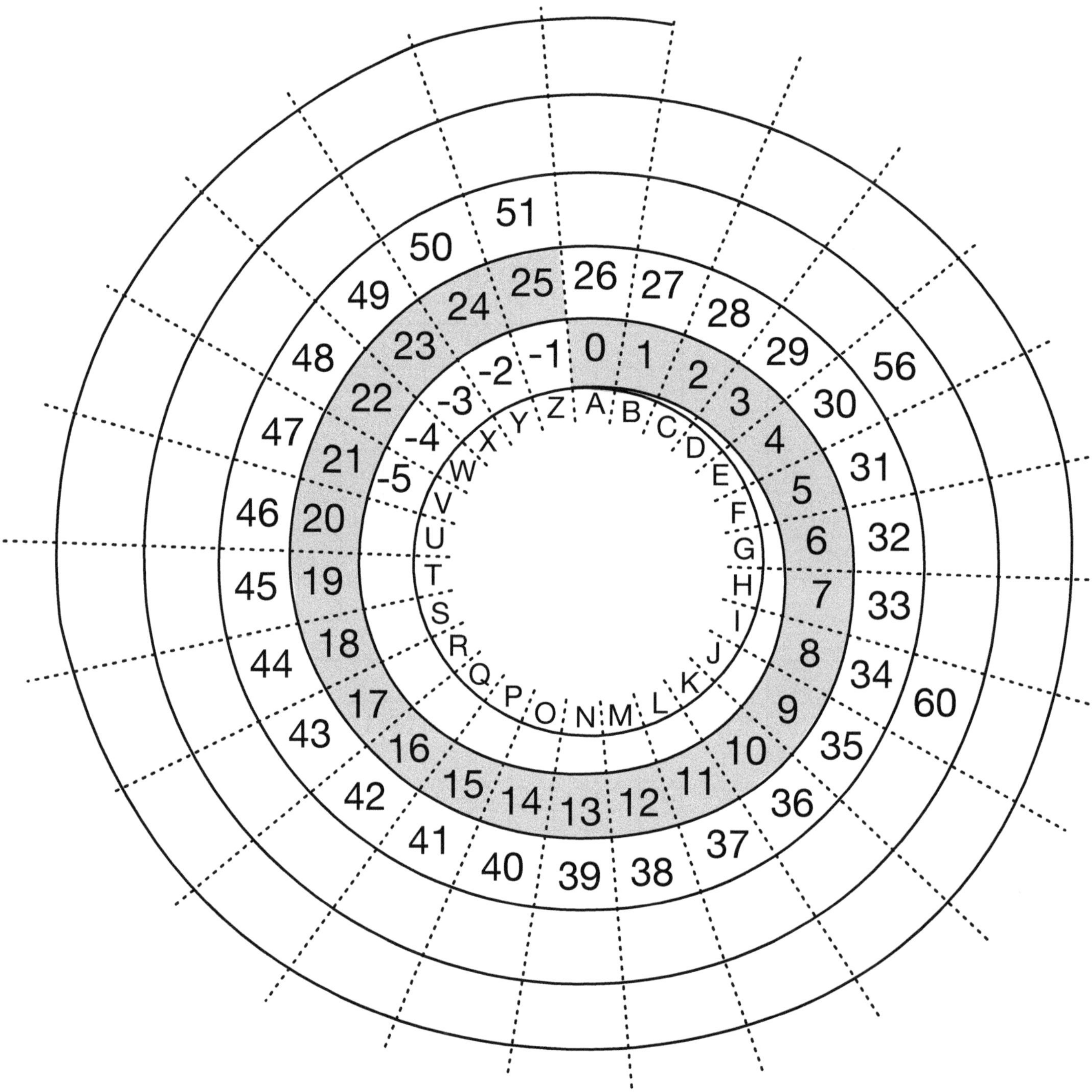

Letter-to-Number Table

a	b	c	d	e	f	g	h	i	j	k	l	m	n	o	p	q	r	s	t	u	v	w	x	y	z
0	1	2	3	4	5	6	7	8	9	10	11	12	13	14	15	16	17	18	19	20	21	22	23	24	25
A	B	C	D	E	F	G	H	I	J	K	L	M	N	O	P	Q	R	S	T	U	V	W	X	Y	Z

Vigenère Square

	a	b	c	d	e	f	g	h	i	j	k	l	m	n	o	p	q	r	s	t	u	v	w	x	y	z
0	A	B	C	D	E	F	G	H	I	J	K	L	M	N	O	P	Q	R	S	T	U	V	W	X	Y	Z
1	B	C	D	E	F	G	H	I	J	K	L	M	N	O	P	Q	R	S	T	U	V	W	X	Y	Z	A
2	C	D	E	F	G	H	I	J	K	L	M	N	O	P	Q	R	S	T	U	V	W	X	Y	Z	A	B
3	D	E	F	G	H	I	J	K	L	M	N	O	P	Q	R	S	T	U	V	W	X	Y	Z	A	B	C
4	E	F	G	H	I	J	K	L	M	N	O	P	Q	R	S	T	U	V	W	X	Y	Z	A	B	C	D
5	F	G	H	I	J	K	L	M	N	O	P	Q	R	S	T	U	V	W	X	Y	Z	A	B	C	D	E
6	G	H	I	J	K	L	M	N	O	P	Q	R	S	T	U	V	W	X	Y	Z	A	B	C	D	E	F
7	H	I	J	K	L	M	N	O	P	Q	R	S	T	U	V	W	X	Y	Z	A	B	C	D	E	F	G
8	I	J	K	L	M	N	O	P	Q	R	S	T	U	V	W	X	Y	Z	A	B	C	D	E	F	G	H
9	J	K	L	M	N	O	P	Q	R	S	T	U	V	W	X	Y	Z	A	B	C	D	E	F	G	H	I
10	K	L	M	N	O	P	Q	R	S	T	U	V	W	X	Y	Z	A	B	C	D	E	F	G	H	I	J
11	L	M	N	O	P	Q	R	S	T	U	V	W	X	Y	Z	A	B	C	D	E	F	G	H	I	J	K
12	M	N	O	P	Q	R	S	T	U	V	W	X	Y	Z	A	B	C	D	E	F	G	H	I	J	K	L
13	N	O	P	Q	R	S	T	U	V	W	X	Y	Z	A	B	C	D	E	F	G	H	I	J	K	L	M
14	O	P	Q	R	S	T	U	V	W	X	Y	Z	A	B	C	D	E	F	G	H	I	J	K	L	M	N
15	P	Q	R	S	T	U	V	W	X	Y	Z	A	B	C	D	E	F	G	H	I	J	K	L	M	N	O
16	Q	R	S	T	U	V	W	X	Y	Z	A	B	C	D	E	F	G	H	I	J	K	L	M	N	O	P
17	R	S	T	U	V	W	X	Y	Z	A	B	C	D	E	F	G	H	I	J	K	L	M	N	O	P	Q
18	S	T	U	V	W	X	Y	Z	A	B	C	D	E	F	G	H	I	J	K	L	M	N	O	P	Q	R
19	T	U	V	W	X	Y	Z	A	B	C	D	E	F	G	H	I	J	K	L	M	N	O	P	Q	R	S
20	U	V	W	X	Y	Z	A	B	C	D	E	F	G	H	I	J	K	L	M	N	O	P	Q	R	S	T
21	V	W	X	Y	Z	A	B	C	D	E	F	G	H	I	J	K	L	M	N	O	P	Q	R	S	T	U
22	W	X	Y	Z	A	B	C	D	E	F	G	H	I	J	K	L	M	N	O	P	Q	R	S	T	U	V
23	X	Y	Z	A	B	C	D	E	F	G	H	I	J	K	L	M	N	O	P	Q	R	S	T	U	V	W
24	Y	Z	A	B	C	D	E	F	G	H	I	J	K	L	M	N	O	P	Q	R	S	T	U	V	W	X
25	Z	A	B	C	D	E	F	G	H	I	J	K	L	M	N	O	P	Q	R	S	T	U	V	W	X	Y

Blank Grid Paper

You can use this page for your own messages.

Cipher Certificate

As you master each cipher, choose a special key for yourself.
Encrypt your name using your special key.

Caesar Cipher

Key ________

your plaintext name																	
your CIPHERNAME																	

Date ______________ *Certified by* ______________________

Additive Cipher

Key ________

your plaintext name																	
your CIPHERNAME																	

Date ______________ *Certified by* ______________________

Keyword Cipher

Keyword ________________ *Keyletter* ________

your plaintext name																	
your CIPHERNAME																	

Date ______________ *Certified by* ______________________

© StudioAZ/Shutterstock.com

Cipher Certificate (continued)

As you master each cipher, choose a special key for yourself.
Encrypt your name using your special key.

Multiplicative Cipher

Key ______

your plaintext name																	
your CIPHERNAME																	

Date ______ *Certified by* ______

Vigenère Cipher

Key ______

your plaintext name																	
your CIPHERNAME																	

Date ______ *Certified by* ______

Affine Cipher

Key (______, ______)

your plaintext name																	
your CIPHERNAME																	

Date ______ *Certified by* ______

© StudioAZ/Shutterstock.com

Cipher Wheels

Directions: *To make a cipher wheel, copy this page onto cardstock and cut out two parts and fasten them together with a brad (paper fastener). Be sure to match the centers carefully so the letters line up properly when the wheel is turned.*

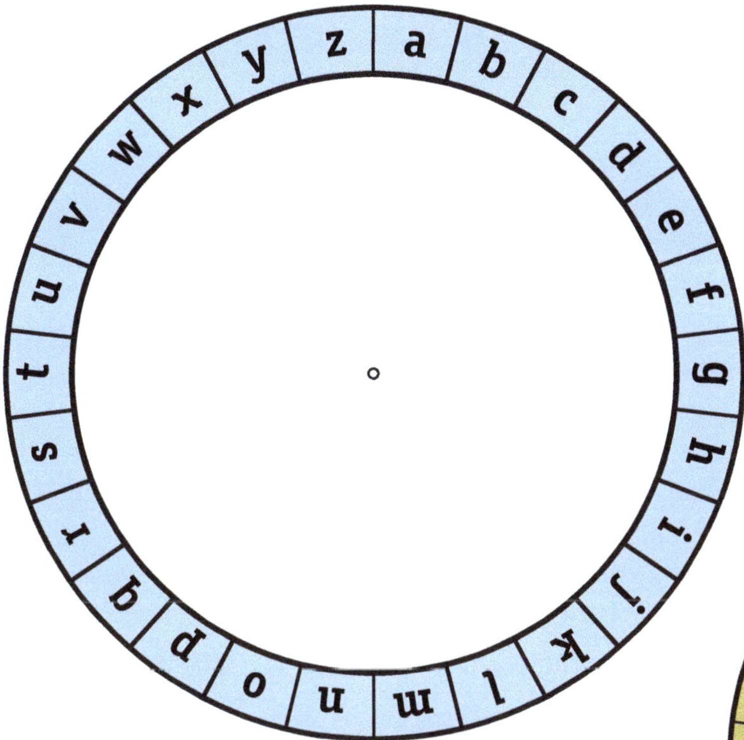

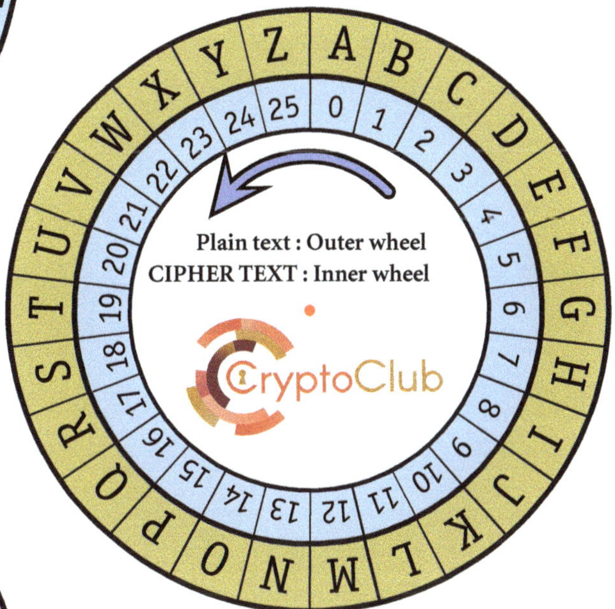

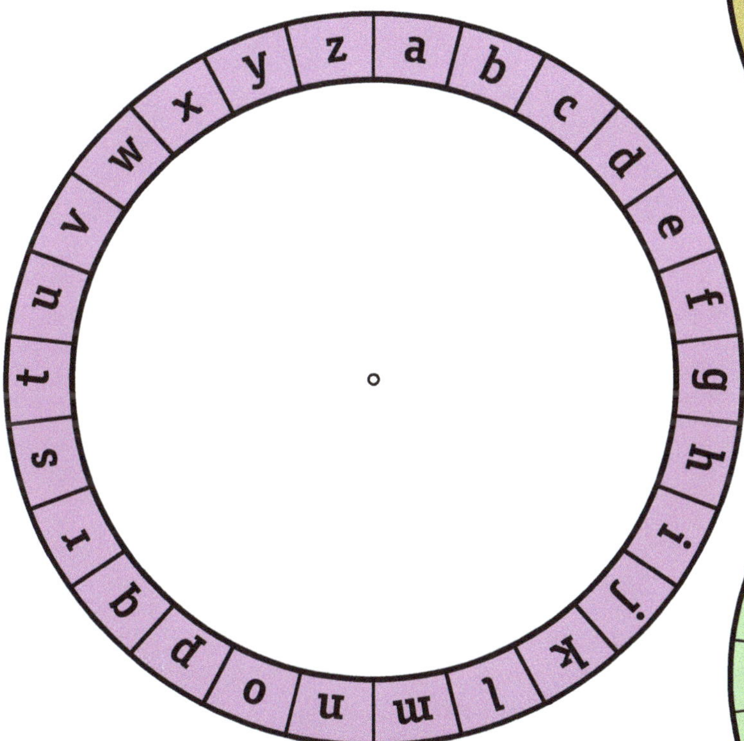

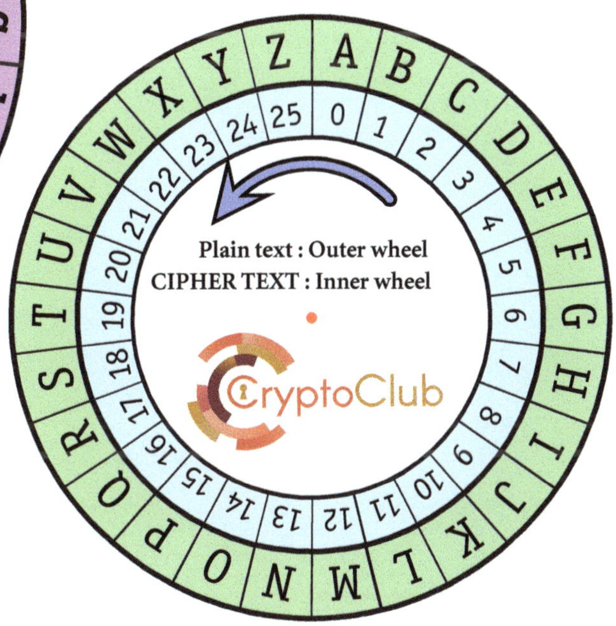

www.ingramcontent.com/pod-product-compliance
Ingram Content Group UK Ltd.
Pitfield, Milton Keynes, MK11 3LW, UK
UKHW052013041026
15590UKWH00008B/2313

9 781792 436512